Secrets of
Western Tantra

OTHER TITLES FROM THE ORIGINAL FALCON PRESS

By Christopher S. Hyatt, Ph.D.
Undoing Yourself With Energized Meditation
Energized Hypnosis (book, audios and videos)
Radical Undoing: The Complete Course for Undoing Yourself (audios &
    videos)
The Psychopath's Bible: For the Extreme Individual
Tantra Without Tears
To Lie Is Human: Not Getting Caught Is Divine

By Christopher S. Hyatt, Ph.D. with Lon DuQuette & Aleister Crowley
Aleister Crowley's Illustrated Goetia

Edited by Christopher S. Hyatt, Ph.D. with contributions by
    Wm. S. Burroughs, Timothy Leary, Robert Anton Wilson et al.
Rebels & Devils: The Psychology of Liberation

By S. Jason Black and Christopher S. Hyatt, Ph.D.
Pacts With the Devil: A Chronicle of Sex, Blasphemy & Liberation
Urban Voodoo: A Beginner's Guide to Afro-Caribbean Magic

By Peter J. Carroll
PsyberMagick
The Chaos Magick Audios

By Antero Alli
Angel Tech: A Modern Shaman's Guide to Reality Selection
Angel Tech Talk (audios)
The 8-Circuit Brain (DVD)

By Israel Regardie
The Complete Golden Dawn System of Magic
What You Should Know About the Golden Dawn
The Golden Dawn Audios
The Eye in the Triangle

By Joseph C. Lisiewski, Ph.D.
Israel Regardie & the Philosopher's Stone
Kabbalistic Handbook for the Practicing Magician
Kabbalistic Cycles & the Mastery of Life
Ceremonial Magic & the Power of Evocation

By Phil Hine
Condensed Chaos: An Introduction to Chaos Magick
Prime Chaos: Adventures in Chaos Magick
The Pseudonomicon

By Steven Heller
Monsters & Magical Sticks: There's No Such Thing As Hypnosis?

By Jay Bremyer
The Dance of Created Lights

For the latest on availability and pricing
visit our website at http://originalfalcon.com

Secrets of Western Tantra

The Sexuality of the Middle Path

Christopher S. Hyatt, Ph.D.

Preface by
Robert Anton Wilson

Introduction by
J. Marvin Spiegelman, Ph.D.

THE *Original* FALCON PRESS
TEMPE, ARIZONA, U.S.A.

International Standard Book Number: 978-1-935150-25-1
Library of Congress Catalog Card Number: 89-81556

First Edition 1989
Second Expanded & Revised Edition 1996
Third Printing 2001
Fourth Printing 2004 (revised)
Fifth Printing 2010

The paper used in this publication meets the minimum requirements of the American National Standard for Permanence of Paper for Printed Library Materials Z39.48-1984

Address all inquiries to:
THE ORIGINAL FALCON PRESS
1753 East Broadway Road #101-277
Tempe, AZ 85282 U.S.A.

(or)
PO Box 3540
Silver Springs, NV 89429 U.S.A.

website: http://www.originalfalcon.com
email: info@originalfalcon.com

ACKNOWLEDGMENTS

I would like to express my gratitude to my dear friend Gary for his energized enthusiasm; and special thanks to Robert Anton Wilson, Arlen Wilson and Joseph Lisiewski for their editorial input and contributions.

I would also like to thank S. Jason Black and Phil Hine for their important contributions.

DEDICATED TO

Dr. Israel Regardie
My teacher and friend

&

Robert Stein, M.D.
One of the greatest analysts who ever lived

TABLE OF CONTENTS

APPENDICES

PREFACE

ROBERT ANTON WILSON

When I was in high school in the late 1940's, I read Robert Graves' "historical grammar of poetic myth," *The White Goddess*. The book left an indelible impression upon me and has influenced everything I have ever written. Women's Liberation (the current bio-social revolutionary force, as distinct from earlier, less radical Feminism) was 20 years in the future then, but I was prepared for most of it by Graves' version of history, in which the Great Goddess, driven underground by Patriarchal religions, survived as the deity of the witches, a figure in folklore (the "fairy godmother"), a perpetual image in art, and the Muse of all true poetry.

About a decade later, in my first published article, "The Semantics of 'God'" (*The Realist*, April 1959) I asked if Divinity should be considered a He, a She or an It, and although I suggested that "it" seemed more appropriate for our scientific age, my second published article, "Joyce and Taoism (*James Joyce Review*, Summer 1959) argued that there was poetic validity in Joyce's and Lao Tse's vision of the Eternal Feminine as the hidden force behind history.

The Valley Spirit never dies:
She is called the Eternal Woman.
  — Lao-Tse, *Tao Te Ching*

In the name of Annah, the Allimaziful, the
Everliving, the bringer of Plurabilities, haloed
be her eve, her singtime sung, her rill be run
unhemmed as it is uneven.
  — James Joyce, *Finnegans Wake*

When I got around to writing my first novel, *Illuminatus!*
(written 1969–70, but not published until 1975) it was the
Great Goddess, in her most mischievous form as Eris (deity
of confusion and chaos), who rises at the climax to strike
down the neo-Nazi villains.

Naturally, when you write about a Jungian archetype,
synchronicities come looking for you. I wrote the above paragraphs yesterday (April 15, 1989), felt unsure that this was
what was appropriate for a preface, and decided to think it
over and start again today. In the evening I looked at a show
about George Washington on Public Television, and James
Flexner, a historian who has written the latest biography of
George, mentioned that the Father of our Country *never used
the word "God"* but did occasionally speak of "Providence."
In referring to Providence, Flexner said, George used different
pronouns at different times, shifting between "He," "She"
and "It."

I immediately remembered my 30-year-old article on "He",
"She" and "It" and was amazed that George Washington,
two hundred years ago, was thinking somewhat like I
thought thirty years ago. The synchronicity was especially
impressive because General Washington is a major character,
perhaps *the* major character, in my novel, *Nature's God* — a
title which comes from Jefferson's *Declaration of Independence*
and strongly implies the same distancing from the Christian
God as Washington's de-genderized and de-personalized
"Providence."

(Jefferson and Washington, like most of the founders of
this Republic, were Deists, and quite suspicious of the
Christian God, a very male "He" with the disposition of an
Absolute Monarch like George III; they preferred the impersonal "Nature's God" or "Providence," an "It" with no more
human motives or passions than the Chinese Tao.)

In *Nature's God*, Adam Weishaupt, founder of the Illuminati, says at one point that the world badly needs "one or two
centuries of brutal materialism" before it can recover from the
"madness" of Christian theology. It is rather odd to recall
that Weishaupt allegedly murdered Washington and served
in his place as President for two terms — according to

Illuminatus! — the fantasy I wrote 19 years ago, which some paranoids have taken seriously, much to my embarrassment.

"Nature's God" or "Providence" — archetypal deist abstractions — were badly needed in the 18th Century to provide a transition from the Christian Era to the materialist era that Darwin would soon unleash upon us. By around 1776 — the year Jefferson wrote the Declaration — Weishaupt founded the Illuminati (to battle "tyranny and superstition," i.e., the Papacy) and Adam Smith published *The Wealth of Nations* — the Christian God was beginning to look a bit absurd to everybody with more than a half inch of forehead. A God who curses the whole human race for the error of two people? And isn't appeased until He murders His own son (who is also Himself, making the deed suicide as well as homicide)? Who impregnates a virgin without damaging the hymen? In Newton's Universe, all this was as incredible (as Jefferson said) "as the three-headed dog of Hades" in Greek mythology.

But Nature's God began to look equally ridiculous, or monstrous, after Darwin ... and it only required Nietzsche, who threw out all the gods (and goddesses) and replaced them with the Will to Power, for the world to be ready for the 20th Century — and barbarism and *anomie* and Existentialism and the Art of the Absurd (the Theatre of Cruelty, surrealism, Black Comedy, Gonzo Journalism and Punk Rock.)

Returning to our first declivity: when Graves dumped The White Goddess, Threefold Muse of Poetry, into my tender adolescent neurons in 1948, I had had about two and a half years to digest the meaning of Hiroshima and Nagasaki. The world itself had had Weishaupt's two centuries of brutal materialism and the results were beginning to look like another nightmare, not an awakening from the Christian nightmare. I began to realize that Nature and Nature's God were cold, inhuman abstractions and that the poet in me needed something more mythic to inspire him to sing, something with deep roots in our psycho-biological being.

In the ten years after Hiroshima, I read a great deal of Carl Jung and came to understand his concept of the Anima — a Goddess who is a permanent part of the human psyche, "inside" each of us, and yet "outside" us also as a vector moving through history. I pondered Jung's hermetic remarks about a possible return of the Goddess in our time. I was startled to find the same thought expressed by Arnold J. Toynbee, a great British historian who predicted the ecological movement and the new (post-1960s) Feminist movement 20 years before they happened. I wrote a long, unpublished essay on *King Kong*, the most haunting film ever made, in which I saw Ann Darrow (Fay Wray) as the Goddess returning to our world and Kong as a pitiful caricature of the solar-phallic, Hercules-Jehovah, Macho Gods of patriarchy, doomed to die atop the Empire State Building, symbol of techno-civilization, as a New Aeon is born. I struggled, painfully and often stupidly, to the awareness that religion, or myths, are metaphors; that they should not be judged in the same terms as scientific models; and that the poet, *not* the rationalist, is the best judge of which metaphors a culture may live richly by and which metaphors are deadly to art and to humanity.

Well, as I say, that was 30 years ago, and all this has become, not the musings of a few poets and Jungians, but a major cultural revolution, and nothing I have written here is really startling anymore. I can only add, for the benefit of those who do not appreciate the accelerations of our time, that, even when thinking these heretical thoughts in the 1940s-1950s, I had no inkling that as the 1980s gave birth to the 1990s there would be a vast audience, not only familiar with such ideas but perhaps already a bit bored with them ...

The Goddess has become so popular, indeed, that recently in New Jersey I heard a prominent Feminist lecture on Her for two hours, and a young (male) neo-Deist actually rose at the end and asked the kind of question that undermined "God" two centuries ago: "Tell me," said he, "Can Goddess create a rock so heavy that She Herself can't lift it?"

Some people will always take metaphors literally, and skeptics like that young man will always be necessary, I guess.

The most important part of *Secrets of Western Tantra* totally transcends such "philosophical" or psychological musings about Nature and Goddess and the Anima, which you can find expressed just as eloquently in dozens of other books currently available. This book goes far beyond theory. It is as practical as a bulldozer and as down-to-earth as a pitchfork. It is not intended to be read merely, but to be *used*.

Dr. Hyatt has decided to publish *real* "Secrets" — techniques of actually transforming yourself from a programmed robot into a self-programmer. Some of these techniques have been around for centuries, and probably for millennia, as closely-guarded "inner-inner teachings" of certain esoteric orders of alchemists and Illuminati. Some of them are very new, and only emerged in recent decades as Dr. Wilhelm Reich's pioneering work on "dissolving the character armor and muscular armor" has been adapted, modified and improved by various *avant garde* psychotherapists and "body workers." As organized by Dr. Hyatt, the corpus of these old and new techniques makes up a curriculum in Self-Liberation absolutely unique in mystical, psychological or philosophical literature: the world's first scientific experimental yoga to be published without expurgating the more controversial (sensory-sensual-sexual) aspects of the Great Work.

Aleister Crowley hinted at much of this — but he only dared to hint, and never wrote all the explicit details. Dr. Reich bluntly declared that his body therapy was intended to liberate the patient from conventional morality — but never published the actual physical details of the work. Dr. Israel Regardie synthesized the best of Crowley and Reich — and a great deal of miscellaneous wisdom acquired elsewhere — but never published the actual details of the physical manipulations that unleash radical body/mind transformation.

What was the fate of these three great prophets? Crowley became the target of what P.R. Stephenson called "a campaign of vilification without precedent in literary history." Reich was kicked out of the International Psychoanalytical Society, the Communist Party, and the Socialist Party, and had his books burned by the U.S. Government. Regardie lived on into a more liberal age, but had learned from the histories of Crowley and Reich and did not test the "liberalism" too much by revealing all he knew.

Dr. Hyatt has decided that the time has come for full disclosure, and I think he is right. There will be howls and anathemas hurled at this book; there will be weeping and gnashing of teeth; there will be the predictable charges of Anarchy and Satanism; but the hour is too late for caution, hermeticism or concealment, all of which have become the habits of the Old Aeon's dying Establishment in seats of power everywhere. The only truly revolutionary act today is to tell the truth about everything.

I hail Dr. Hyatt for his wisdom, but even more I hail him for his courage.

Like a loaded gun, this book should be treated with great respect. You are not dealing with mere "ideas" here. You hold in your hands the keys to actual changes in your self and in your relations with every man, every woman and every sentient being in space-time. If it took courage to publish this, as it did, it will take intelligence to use it properly. Every copy should be labeled, "Handle With Care."

Robert Anton Wilson
Los Angeles, 16 April 1989

INTRODUCTION

J. MARVIN SPIEGELMAN, Ph.D.
Jungian Analyst

While reading about the three experiences that Dr. Hyatt had of the Goddess I chanced to look up for the moment in my pleasant patio, and saw a tiny lady bug, scurrying quickly along the ground toward my foot. I put my finger in front of her and she determinedly climbed aboard. I made it possible for her to rest on Hyatt's manuscript and she did so, peacefully and contentedly, it seemed to me. I could then see the interesting markings on her shiny red back: four black dots, arranged in a square. For me this was a synchronicity, a meaningful coincidence, which I took as a benevolent mark of Her presence. In my understanding, this mandala, a symbol of wholeness, appearing on this gentle and widely appreciated "lady bug", was an emblematic expression of the rightness of Hyatt's efforts and a validation, in my eyes, for his service to the Self as it appears in feminine form. I presented my interpretation of this event, silently, to the Goddess as manifested in this gentle bug, and asked if my understanding was correct. It seemed to me that she bowed, ever so subtly, and gracefully flew away, to "her children" no doubt — to her many creative followers (like Hyatt) who are "burning" with passion in Her service.

I have known Hyatt for quite a long time, (more than twenty years), and have seen him in many incarnations — in this life — as student, psychotherapist, director of clinics, investment counselor, publisher, writer, Mage, as well as in the non-role manifestations of expert sailor, street-smart battler, "stand-in" for Orson Welles. I was one of the three people who referred him to Dr. Israel Regardie, who plays

such an important role in the "third" manifestation of the
Goddess, mentioned by Hyatt.

Yet all my knowledge of him did not give me an adequate
understanding of his fierce battle against pomposity and
hypocrisy, against authoritarianism and cant. This book,
especially the experiences of the Goddess, helps me very
much more, in this regard. I can now see his battle as his
service to the Goddess, his dedication and devotion to the
overcoming of the rigidity of a patriarchal condition which
has seen its twilight, leading to an elevation of the feminine
principle and all that entails in the way of appreciation rather
than repression of the instincts, and an ethic to match.

Hyatt's Kundalini vision of Christ with the Nun taking the
watch from his wrist, also helped me to understand the
antagonism he has expressed — as he often does in this
book — towards Christianity. I had often mentioned to him
that I had experienced any number of Christian clergy, nuns,
and lay persons, of outstanding qualities — humanity, toler-
ance, intelligence and humor — and that this particular
branch of the "chosen of God," the Christian, surely deserved
better treatment. He would then detail to me a story of the
Christian record of repression, intolerance, stupidity, violence,
hate, etc. which were just the opposite of what I had experienced, but which I could not gainsay. All that belonged to the
decaying patriarchy, I would say, and we would agree.

But now I see that the figure of Christ is, indeed, terribly
important for Hyatt, and even in his fury he bows his head to
this incarnation of the divine. In Hyatt's vision, Christ gently
and benevolently allows the nun to take the watch from his
wrist; he is in no way the authoritarian and cruel figure that
oppresses the feminine. Thus, I would say, Hyatt is participating in this handing over of power and value, and it may
even be his own very powerful patriarchal energies which are
both battling and participating in this changeover. It would
seem, therefore, that this excellent book, focusing on transformation, rather than repression or sublimation, is a true
symbolic outcome of the developmental process and is useful
to all who need to transform, particularly men. "We shall
overcome" was spoken not only for repressed African-

Americans, but to all of those unable to develop in our aeon-ending culture. Hyatt's service, therefore, is blessed by the Goddess, as the lady-bug showed me.

It is quite flattering to me, of course, that he chooses to make use of my psychological comments about the various chakras in Kundalini Yoga. My own understanding, naturally, derives from the work of Arthur Avalon and of C.G. Jung, as well as the authorities that they mention, so it is gratifying to see one's own efforts linking up with the positive patriarchy continuing with the next generation. (Not all fathers are authoritarian.) Hyatt's work makes creative use of this material, along with the neo-Reichian methods developed by Israel Regardie.

I am particularly impressed with how Hyatt has combined various sources in a creative and practical way. I am familiar with the neo-Reichian exercises which assist in the reduction of tension and increase sensory awareness. I can also attest that disciplined activity along these lines produces the kinds of relaxation and energy-consciousness that are claimed. The combination of these with the magical methods of meditation, such as the Middle Pillar, was a highlight of the achievements of Regardie, and these are well-recognized. Hyatt has extended this syncretic work considerably by placing it all in a context of Western Tantra which, he calls "the sexuality of the Middle Path." I am sure that he looks forward to hearing how his own experimentation is received and furthered by others.

This is no mere "how to" book, however. Hyatt's attitude, despite his antagonism to dogmatic "faiths," is both religious and respectful. For example, when he insists that all of this work is in the service of transcendence, he says:

> ... it matters not whether eating or sex or opening a door with your right hand is transcended; what matters is that consciousness becomes fully aware that transcendence is possible. My position has sometimes been regarded as amoral or immoral by conventional western religions. On the lower planes of man's functioning as an insect, this is no doubt correct. On the higher planes, however, this position is highly moral.

Hyatt's, work, therefore, is far from being merely self-indulgent. Indeed, he is just as uncompromising about his own "shadow," as we Jungians call the less savory aspects of ourselves, as he is about the hypocrisy mentioned earlier. To undertake the program he proposes about self-transformation, followed by the joint process of transformation and the production of the "magickal child," would obviously require qualities of honesty, persistence, devotion and care which no mere hedonist could endure for more than five minutes.

I hope that Dr. Hyatt will receive thoughtful consideration for his ideas and suggestions and that readers will undertake the experiments proposed in the spirit with which he offers them. His unique combination of perspectives and methods of quite diverse origin, along with precise practical application, merits this consideration. One hopes that he will be rewarded with responses from others which will help him extend and refine his views.

CHAPTER ONE

A NEW SEXUAL ECOLOGY[1]

History does not repeat itself. Human behavior does. If we wish to change future history then we must change human behavior. Man is a foetus yet unborn. Unless he is freed from his notions of sin and from compulsive and ordinary sexuality the foetus will die undelivered.
— Dr. Christopher S. Hyatt speaking with
Dr. Israel Regardie, Summer 1983.

THE SEXUALITY OF THE MIDDLE PATH

I call what follows the sexuality of the Middle Path. Its purpose is to help transform the Planet through intelligent and joyous sexual practices. It is a sexuality for the future — *NOW*.

I use the phrase *Middle Path* to differentiate this theory and method from normal forms of sexual practice, which broadly fit the categories of restraint or indulgence.

From the beginning of time the human race has attempted to elevate itself from its animal ancestry. The methods it has used have worn themselves out at best and failed at worst. Moral dictates, self-hate, in(dull)gence, have all proven inadequate and dangerous. The time has come when something else is needed. Something which acknowledges and respects the animal side of our nature and fully recognizes our God-Goddess qualities. Without this dual acknowledgment man

---

[1]Ecology: the conservation of natural resources, pollution control, survival studies, the study of eco-systems, the human environment — methods of ensuring the future(s) of an environment and a new race of wo/man.

and the planet seem doomed to regression and possible destruction. We must give up our outmoded hive learning devices of self-hate and restriction as methods of control and transcendence. Terror and punishment do not lend themselves to creating useful, joyful, flexible, intelligent human beings.

ULTIMATE JOY THROUGH DISCIPLINE

Middle Path sexuality is neither indulgence nor abstinence but ultimate joy through discipline.

Unlike most forms of Tantric practice, orgasm is not only allowed but *essential* to create the desired results. Avoiding orgasm is a No-No for Western Tantra.

MELTING & GIVING

Many forms of Tantra are restrictive and limiting, focusing on holding back and holding in. Western Tantra is completely different. Its focus is on melting and giving, using only small amounts of holding to make the Gift more beautiful and complete. Western Tantra holds the belief that complete Orgasm is freeing, and energizing. In fact, the methods are designed with that result in mind.

The outcome of following the creative and liberating path of Middle Path Sexuality (MPS) is enlightenment and the creation of what I term the Magickal Child. This "Child", whether physical or spiritual will become the leading edge of the new human race the planet is creating. The planet is now beginning to accelerate its plans for Quality.

The process is somewhat demanding and is not designed for the average student, but for those who have the persistence and determination to *work hard with joy* to achieve their goals of flexibility, increased intelligence and enlightenment.

While I spend some time on theory and definition, the *soul of this book will be found in the methods and techniques.* I stress this because there has been so much written on theory and so little given on reaching the goals promised by Tantric practices. If you find the theory and explanations annoying, tedious, or uninteresting, ignore them for the time being. Get into the practice sessions at once.

The proof of this is simple: *anyone who practices these methods will achieve the same results whether or not she knows anything of the history and theory of the methods herein described. The theory and history serve both as motivation and a stimulant to the conscious mind of the participants.*

The methods described herein are a form of bio-psycho-spiritual sexuality. It is biological, being rooted in "natural" sexuality and body-awareness. It is psychological, in releasing one from inhibition and compulsion. It is "spiritual" in transforming consciousness into dimensions unknown to "ordinary" (domesticated) humanity. It is a form of what I believe Tantra to be; however, what is different is that it is both conscious and unconscious. It includes control, the will, great discipline and the greatest pleasures.

While developing discipline and will, following the course of (MPS) is also a great Initiation. Anyone who religiously practices these techniques and methods becomes initiated into the most ancient and powerful mystical order on the planet. The name of this Order is Alpha-Omega, and its purpose is conscious evolution. Its method is to use the power of "instinct" to free ourselves from the automatisms of "instinct" and create the new man-woman — the new Adam.

ORGASTIC THUNDER

What follows is the sexuality of enlightenment without giving up the joy of orgasm. In fact, complete orgastic release is essential if the goal of conscious evolution is to be satisfied.

The form of sexuality described in this book is beyond anything known, yet it has been with us in disguised, and not so disguised, forms from the beginning of awareness.

What is new are the methods. THE NUTS AND BOLTS are revealed here for the first time. Nothing is held back. The 21st century is upon us and it is time for new forms of sexual practice.

My hope is that this work will bring a new option for individuals. Instead of the ordinary forms of sexuality we practice, I provide a method for the Intelligent Adolescent.

What follows is a sexuality for a lifetime and as you will see a sexuality for eternity.

CHAPTER TWO
SEX ON THE PLANET

The sexual or orgastic response is one of the most powerful forces on the Planet. It keeps everything going and everything alive. It is a Power of great Joy and great Pain for both the Planet and all its inhabitants.

It is the source of death, pain, misery and suffering.
It is the source of birth, joy, creation and happiness.

It has been regulated, discussed, dissected, divided and worshipped from the time when people first discovered its pleasures, its powers and its terrors.

Sex has always been associated with death, violence, re-birth, good and evil. Empires have been built on it; others have been destroyed because of it.

Fortunes are won and lost on it. Lives, both collectively and personally, have been built on it and demolished by it.

Marriages are made on it and lost on it.

Its powers and forces bring together and rip apart.

One hour doesn't go by in which we are not both reminded of it and told not to be taken in by it.

Attraction between the sexes has created giant industries, and without it, there would be nothing.

All religions are based on it in one way or another.

Freud built his theory on it. Physicists discuss the attraction and repulsion of charged particles.

What is this power which men and women desire, worship and fear? What is so important about it? How can a moment

24

of pleasure have caused so much grief and concern? It has made men and women both adversaries and friends.

Sex is described by so many words, yet no one can explain an orgasm to anyone else. Why does sex need to be so pleasurable? Would humans and other animals fail to reproduce their own kind if it wasn't? Would the human race die out if all the taboos placed on sex didn't exist? Is it the taboos which keep us interested and excited? Is it the violation of Taboo which drives us to the extremes we go through? Is it the suggestiveness of the use of clothes? What is it, that can simultaneously provide so much pleasure and so much pain and misery (i.e., wars, over-population, starvation, crime, and the possible destruction of Planet Earth)?

Must sex be compulsive in order for us to be so irrational as to bring another human in the world to suffer and die?

Procreation is the most selfish act in the world. We bring other humans into the world to take our place. We create a phantom personal immortality. What if we were immortal? Would we want children?

What if sex were not pleasurable at all? Would it still be popular. How many children would there be?

Is the sexual instinct and its expression a big joke on rational/conscious man? After all, anyone can do it. Anyone can make children. Anyone can and will be a god to these children. Are our egos so weak we need children to look up to us or do we reproduce because we can't we help it? Is that why sex is such a mystery to civilized man? Why is it so private? Does it inflate us to think that our sexuality is so different from animals' (and it is), or is it that the mere idea of it reminds us that our will and consciousness are but pawns of this great ANIMAL POWER?

Must sex always be, like King Kong, a raw ANIMAL POWER running amok in our "civilized" world?

I do not know the answers to these and many other questions. I do not even know if these are "real" questions, deserving to be considered intelligently.

What I do know is that if Sex is the most powerful force on the planet, (or even if it ranks in the top three), then until IT is transformed, the world's peoples and the planet will not be transformed and now live in mortal danger.

Many methods have been developed to control, transform and regulate the sexual force. Each of them has failed, creating more misery in its wake. No one alive knows what "natural" sex is for Humans. We have been too "civilized" (domesticated). We think that our own sexual preferences and habits are enlightened, when in most cases, they are a result of our genes and of being born into a particular civilization and time. We have the hubris to believe that the opposites of abstinence and indulgence are the only two poles which exist on the sexual discrimination scale.

We have Dionysian indulgence as one morality.

We have Christian abstinence as another.

"Christ versus Dionysus" was Nietzsche's motto. Even he, who challenged most dualisms, did not challenge this one: he chose Dionysus.

But there is also marriage, monotheistic style.

And there is marriage, polytheistic style.

There is marriage and affairs.

There is marriage and swinging.

There is living together.

There is spiritual sex with no orgasm, as in Hindu Tantra.

There are other Tantras of one flavor or another. In fact Tantra as we use the term has nothing to do with what most people call sex. Tantra is Meta-Sex.

There are "perversions" of one type or another.

There are fetishes: leather, chains, "cross dressing," etc.

There are male/female sexual happenings.

There are female/female, male/male relations etc.

Then there are techniques, which include various orifices and body parts.

The list goes on and on. There is every combination in the world including sex with oneself.

All of this however, has not led to transformation either individually or collectively. We simply have different forms of the same thing.

Everything under the sun has been tried, except to, my knowledge, what follows in this book. A New Sexual Ecology is Being Born.

LOVE & SEX: THE REAL TABOO

To paraphrase Dr. Robert Stein, (1974) from his fascinating book *Incest and Human Love,* when a culture becomes preoccupied with inhibiting and controlling the instinctual forces of life, which of course includes sexuality, we can assume that its methods of coping with the incest taboo are also inadequate. In other words the culture's social institutions are failing.

If we combine this idea with Michel Foucault's notion that "sexuality" evolves from the need of the power structure to control sex for its own economic and political purposes, we are left with a sorry state of affairs.

This sorry state of affairs is known as splitting. What I mean here is that sex and love have a difficult time in finding complete unified expression. (This work attempts to address this situation.)

From Stein's point of view this is the way a culture copes with the incest taboo, and from Foucault's it is the way a culture channels sex for its own purposes of power.

In other words, love is *disconnected* from sex in Western Civilization. We have been told that sex and love should be *one,* but not as an experience — rather as a state of *law.* In this sense we are left with sex as reproduction and loveless compulsion. Marriage is designed as a unit of reproduction for the purposes of creation and consumption. The true expression of love and sex are secondary — left in the realm of romantic fantasy, a hope or a dream.

It is truly infrequent in this culture that the depths of both the love and sex instincts are felt completely. When they are both felt deeply, and remember, this is always inhibited by the incest taboo and the assumption that a commitment is neces- sary, we have complete orgastic love.

Conversely, compulsive sexuality is an attempt to free sex from the purposes of reproduction and social control. However, it too is devoid of true Union, as deep love has a forced association with the necessity of a commitment. Would orgastic love be felt more readily if commitment were not an obligation, not a "law" indoctrinated since infancy?

Compulsive sexuality also serves to demonstrate the "failure" of our culture in controlling the fear of incest. Instead of addressing incest, it has addressed sexuality itself, thus confounding us to believe that the "awful" effects of incest are co-extensive with sex itself. How does our culture differentiate sex from incest? In fact it does not address this issue in a conscious manner at all, but allows the unconscious to deal with the problem. Thus sex and love are split in practice, although frequently alive in fantasy. We have been taught that the deep love we felt as children toward our parents "must not" be associated with sex and the sex we felt during our adolescence "must not" be associated with love.

The culture then assumes that upon marriage or commit- ment the union of these two instincts will automatically take place. I have been kind in making this last statement. More correctly it doesn't care. Its purpose is to create more orderly producers and consumers.

The practice of Western Tantra outlined in this book is a powerful method of bringing love and sex back together with- out the *obligation* of commitment as instilled by our culture. The only commitment is to the Third principle in Tantra — the God-Form — the Essence. It is transpersonal. By this I do not mean that a couple should not have a commitment to each other, but that the WORK doesn't require ordinary forms of commitment. What it requires is the desire that sex and love be one as an experience. This is accomplished when there is orgastic response and not a mere sexual response.

Western Tantra heals the mind/body split by allowing the true nature and power of instinct to live. When we do this, Instinct itself is transformed and the true gifts of human life become accessible. The fear of being overwhelmed or taken over by the power of the instincts no longer terrifies the individual who is then free to consciously participate in his or her own evolution. Repression and denial are replaced with differentiation. This creative function also allows us to see the true nature of instincts. Instead of perceiving them as being opposed to consciousness and civilization as we have been taught from the Christian-Judeo world-view, we see them as the loving root from which rationality itself springs.

We begin to see our development and yearn for the opportunity to embrace our multiplicity in a more holistic fashion, and the world of either/or becomes the greatest fiction.

LOVE, DEATH & SEX: ANOTHER TABOO

True orgastic bliss is very similar to death. The only reason death should be feared is that most people have never lived. Joy in death, letting go completely, is akin to the results obtained by practicing Western Tantra. However, orgastic bliss can only be experienced if love and sex become one. Much like love and sex have been split in the Western world, life and death have been split. Complete orgasm embraces and heals the splits between life/death and sex/love. Once the healing has occurred the need for and dependence on ordinary religion also vanishes. Thus the priests and the politicians have fought hard against the orgastic response. This is even true of many forms of Eastern Tantra, as well as the ancient Kabbalists who realized the power and implications of the sex act. (However, both groups demand the giving up of pleasure, and/or the sanction of the priest.)

Western Tantra as described in this book demands neither. It combines aspects of the Kabbalah with the discipline of Eastern Tantra. More importantly it provides the methods necessary for freeing the body/mind from the pains and chains of early training. Thus it functions first as an Opening, then a Meditation and then Death. The Death I speak of is the Death of Union, where all division merges back into itself.

Complete orgasm is a Death. Complete orgasm is a Birth. Complete orgasm is Life.

Western Tantra is a means of returning to the awareness of the Primal Urge, the Alpha — Ain Soph, the creator of form.

Form becomes a deadly illusion when it "acts" as if it **is** the Essence. Form is simply the playground of the *silent beginnings. The Essence can not be known. It is not part of the Time-Space continuum.*

When form "thinks" itself the essence, then it is time for it to dissolve. Complete orgasm takes one back to the "beginnings" — the primal urge of unity desiring to know itself through its possibilities. When form, be it a person or a social institution is *willing* to let go — to die, then death is not painful. Pain is a result of a struggle, the belief that the form **is** the essence.

All of the exercises and methods in this book are forms designed to help you reach the point of complete, chaotic orgasm, the creative force of life itself. But remember, the forms are *NOT* the orgasm.

These forms, these methods, are necessary. They help you Undo the identifications which you have learned. Dr. Regardie used to say that when a student studies the Kabbalah he begins to believe in the validity of its categories. If he studies enough and studies well, all the categories collapse. In this sense, and in this sense *only*, does he experience a Satori. From this point of view Kabbalah is like Zen. However, the danger is that most students do not get past the first few steps.

Death in the sense that Westerners view it is an illusion. This illusion results from believing the form to be the essence. This is a necessary device by which Spirit enjoys itself. However, the forming process and the disintegration process are *only process.* They are not things. Death as we understand it can only happen to things, not to processes. Ultimate orgasm removes the Thingness from life and throws you back to the Primal Process — The No-Thing.

All form is necessary as part of the process of experience. The danger lies only in losing awareness that form is simply form — the way in which the Essence knows and experiences its Infinite Possibilities. In Spiritual as well as Mundane matters humans have the awful tendency of really believing that the form is the essence. One doesn't have to look far to find this. Churches, governments, families, jobs, words all are forms which have been mistaken for the Essence. Unless this process is slowed down or more deeply understood, man himself will become *more of a thing* to be processed and engineered in service of the Form. This is the true Fall, believing words are knowledge and that knowledge is Essence. An interesting way of understanding that the form is not the essence is the following model.

The shell of an egg contains the living primal force. The shell is also an aspect of that primal force. If the shell is too hard the new being can not break out. If the shell is too soft the new being cannot be protected. The image of a new being emerging from the shell is the image I would like you to keep in mind. Get a feeling of this image. Now imagine that you are breaking out. Use the shell as food as energy to help you reach the next step. As *YOU* reach the next step do not allow the new shell that you have created along the way to hold you back. Break out of it. Let go of it. Emerge again, again and again. Once you believe that the shell you have made along the journey *is the primal force then you are no longer alive.*

CHAPTER THREE
SECRETS OF WESTERN TANTRA

I have borrowed from many traditions which have attempted to claim absolute knowledge and authority concerning this topic. Therefore, I apologize in advance for disrupting their claim to absolute knowledge and authority. For those who are followers of these dogmatic systems, I can understand your frustration with me, but I will not be restrained by grunts and groans. I do provide very specific methods which can be removed from the models I use to explain this endeavor. The beauty of this system is that you do not have to believe in it for it to work. This, for me, is a sign of its efficaciousness and elegance.

Finally, I hope the reader will not be put off from the methods because of my bias to communicate them in the form which suits my own consciousness, history and emotional needs.

COOPERATION

Tantra is the sexuality of Co-operation: first within self, then between selves and then joined with the Goddess. Tantra is Love and Power in Harmony. It is the Power of Love Melting.

Thus Tantra stresses harmony Within, Between and With. **It is Non-Competitive.**

COMMUNICATION

Tantra is the ultimate form of Communication and Awareness. Human difficulties stem from *a lack of awareness that communication has broken down.* Once awareness dawns, then proper steps can be taken to establish harmonious and productive communication within the self, between selves and with the Mother of Life.

Awareness that a difficulty or a desire exists is *both* the *FIRST* and *NECESSARY* step for change. Most humans are not aware of their ignorance. However, they credit themselves as being aware when in fact they are sound asleep. This might be best understood if you think of the mind as a tape recorder. A tape recorder doesn't have to be aware that it is a tape recorder to perform its function. Nor does it have to know how it works. Neither does it need to know what is recorded on it or how it got there. It simply does its job. A human being is different from a tape recorder in the sense that it vigorously defends itself from being erased. One reason why it does this is because it believes that its recordings are its soul, its essence. The human being responds to awareness as an attack against its essence or self-esteem. Awareness means looking at one's self from another vantage point without being judgmental. It is pure witnessing. This can be very painful because the rudimentary form of awareness is always comparative and judgmental.

Awareness develops by comparisons. The mind compares itself to some standard or ideal which also has been recorded. Now the mind evaluates whether or not it has measured up. If it hasn't measured up it tries to make changes by whatever means it has been taught. The ordinary way of doing this is to attack. Any attack is usually met with a counter-attack. The end result is usually frustration, depression followed by denials and excuses. This entire process is NOTHING BUT a model. It is learned and it serves the purpose of keeping the person "safely" asleep. Change in this fashion is at best slow, unnecessarily painful and haphazard.

When two or more people get together the same process takes place. Each person secretly compares him/herself to the other. Each rates the other on internal scales of worth and value. Each concludes how they stack up and then the process of attack and counterattack begin. Who is more beautiful? Who is smarter? Who is more holy? Who is more sophisticated? Who is more clever? Who is more wealthy? Who is stronger? Who is weaker? These and many other comparisons are made. Relational maps are drawn from these comparisons. One of the first maps is the denial that such comparisons are taking place at all. To admit this is a sign that one is vulnerable. To admit vulnerability to oneself or another is a loss of worth. The process goes on and on. No wonder there is so little Love, understanding and communication in the world. No wonder people are unhappy and miserable. Tantra does away with all of this non-sense.

ORDER & CHAOS

A number of points which differentiate this form of Tantra from all others is the juxtaposition of complete order and control with total orgastic chaos. What we mean by chaos here is complete loss of control. We learn control to lose Control. Chaos is simply the principle of Indeterminacy. Thus we have an integration of two extremes leading to the ultimate Tantric dance. *This is the Power of Love Melting. It is our chance for Intimacy with the Unknown. This can only happen when we let go of our sense of "individuality."*

REVELATION IN THE NOW
THE WITNESSING OF THE IMPERSONAL

The purpose of Western Tantra is to purify the psycho-spiritual system by synergistically combining "masculine" activity (YANG) with "feminine" passivity (YIN). Through the practices described in this text the reader will note that the author urges a form of "mixing" of these male and female energies. This is accomplished by direct sexual practices which release the super-human energy Hindus call Kundalini, culminating in orgastic bliss. The mixing of sexual powers in a controlled fashion is designed to impart to each participant the qualities of his/her opposite energy. This in turn breaks open the shell of our confinement and allows us to witness the vital energy of the Impersonal working through our form. I call this *Revelation in the Now*.

Thus for the male, female qualities are implanted and for the female, male qualities are implanted. For those who have received this dual quality of consciousness a new life springs forth from the deep and exalted roots of the Lotus.

Kundalini is action. It is the roots of the male and female flower divided by the Act of the Goddess making Herself known to Herself, reaching out with conscious intention to re-unite in bliss. Thus the pain of division is redeemed by the joy of union. In this sense, the trauma of creation is healed, allowing the world to leap into its next stage of evolution. It is the dance of the moment.

This "sexual-spiritual-mixing" makes each participant whole by rendering duality conscious. Thus, the male active principle is "tempered" by the female passive power, giving him a deeper and wider perspective of life, and of course the female also acquires the benefit of expansion from the addition of the "male" qualities.

The feminization of the masculine and the masculization of the feminine creates a sweetness and tenderness beyond mere description, without losing clarity and strength. This results from the *Melting* process. As melt down takes places the window of the Divine is Opened.

The "new" being who arises from these practices also possesses great powers of healing, whether in the practice of medicine, psychotherapy, or the laying on of hands. It has been long known that the best healers possess the strength and integrated qualities of both sexes. (This is why Jesus and others are so often portrayed as epicene.) Here, at last, is a method which makes this a living reality.

Through long preparation and intense practice the forces of power which arise from below allow the aspirant to know her/his true nature. The focus of identity reformulates itself from those received by culture and training, to those more Primal (the original Sparks of Existence). These acts of conse-cration give the aspirant direct access to the mysteries of life which have been clouded by illusions and form.

The essence of all great religious and esoteric orders is the regulation of the psycho-sexual powers. These can be absti-nence for the priest and procreative indulgence for the flock, as in the Catholic regime; promiscuity of the pagan or hedonic cults; missionary sexuality of the Protestant, temporally controlled sexuality of the religious Jew; the Tantric practices of the Hindu; marital sexuality; and numerous modern practices such as group sex, "one night stands", yuppie sex, mate swapping, affairs, etc. Except for the Hindu practices and some of the ancient pagan rituals, the remaining forms of sexual regulation are disguises and nonsense born of fear, ignorance, repression and the slave mandate. ✓

Many secret religious orders had as their foundation the practice of sacred sexual acts. However, many of them, including the Golden Dawn, disguised these practices for obvious reasons (fear of the church and state) — or, which is more likely, had forgotten that they even existed.

Many proponents of the Golden Dawn and related traditions, like Waite and Felkins, were so "Christianized" that they were even sex negative, attempting to live the life of the Puritan and of course influencing modern occultism in an ascetic direction. Others, like Crowley and Regardie, preserved the essence of the ancient order, knowing that the proper use of the Psycho-Sexual brought true enlightenment. This is why Dr. Regardie felt that Reich's therapy was the best therapy for the aspiring student. However, he knew that while Reich's therapy would lead to a form of orgastic potency, it would never lead to true enlightenment. Reich himself had no use for Eastern practices, which of course included Yoga. Regardie often told me that Reich must have known of Tantra, or if he didn't he should have.

SEXUALITY IN WESTERN CULTURE

Historically in Western Culture, Sexuality has been compulsive. Our tradition either preaches abstinence and restraint, or indulgence and impulsiveness, and sometimes both at the same time (the wife for children, the prostitute for release). These are the two paths of ordinary sexuality which of course most participants believe to be extraordinary. In fact most people believe that their form of sexual behavior is unique and complete and from an ordinary point of view this is true.

In the earlier stages of marriage, sexuality was adapted to serve as a "bonding" device. It was hoped that by initially prescribing pre-marital restraint, and then sanctioning marital indulgence, a pleasure bond *imprint* would occur which would glue the couple together to insure that the infant would survive *in the way* the religious-cultural paradigm sees as the *only possible way* to preserve itself and the species. (For any culture the notion of the human species and itself are the *SAME*.)

As history shows, virginity often served to create a powerful post-coital bonding and as an economic device for those patriarchal systems in which ownership was regarded as the highest expression of prestige and power.

Most early phases of Western civilization (to 1960) showed little care for the nature and nurture of female sexuality. This is in stark contrast to the ancient female mystery cults where female sexual enjoyment was paramount, and in some cases men were "used" as sexual objects, much as women have been used more recently.

The male religions as well as most of their secret orders have persisted in punishing the female for the knowledge and power she possessed regarding the sublime use of psycho-sexual powers. She has always been closer to this truth than her patriarchal male counter parts. They not only feared her knowledge but her sexual abilities. Thus they created the image (and partial reality) that females were primarily "uninterested in sex."

In terms of sexual capability the male is significantly weaker. His sensitivity to sexual criticism has led to much of the "contempt" (disguised fear) he feels toward the "weaker sex."

DIVISION & CONFLICT
THE MULTIPLE BRAIN
THE SEXES & BRAIN WARS

The division of the sexes with its hierarchical form of dominance and subservience is similar to the division enforced by culture on the brain. Here I am not talking about left brain or right brain, but among the reptile brain, the mammalian brain and the neo-cortex.

Humans possess at least "three brains" — the reptile brain, the old mammal brain and the new brain. Each brain has its own peculiar way of operating and its own sense of self. We might characterize these brains as the Rigid Brain (reptile), the Oscillating Brain (mammalian, emotional, hooked to pleasure and pain), and the Planning Brain (which includes the frontal lobes, the most recent development, and the so-called right and left hemispheres) and is concerned with ideas, time, inventions, plans, values and culture. One of the primary activities of the cortex is to INHIBIT.

INHIBITION & CHOICE

Reptiles simply survive. To a large extent they do not play, like dogs and cats, nor can they easily delay or inhibit their reactions. Dogs and cats play, but to a large extent do not invent, although they have a greater capacity to inhibit their responses. In essence both groups can not go beyond what they are. Humans can go beyond their primal brains by using their complicated cortex. One way they do this is by learning how to DELAY certain actions.

Technically this is called Inhibition. Humans not only can inhibit or delay certain older brain activities, they can also inhibit cortical activity, thus giving us the appearance of choice and free will. Choice and decision thus require delay or inhibition. Each choice often means that something else must be delegated to another time; thus humans are known as a time binding species in conflict.

Another function of DELAY is that it stimulates the brain to begin the process of association and network building. The secret for "happy/creative brain play is in learning *HOW* to Delay. Very few cultures have incorporated creative delay into their reality formula. They teach Delay by employing fear and trembling and then labeling it Morality, implying a mandate of Heavenly necessity. This primitive form of enforced evolution is the only meaningful purpose of early "morality."

Reptiles are not in conflict within themselves, nor are cats. Reptiles do not hate themselves, nor do dogs. Nor do these animals make war on themselves. This is so because they do not have visions. They do not have ideals or goals for which to strive. In this sense their future does not determine their present. Man's goals, wishes and *future* can determine his present.

The cortex can not only determine the WAY something from the lower brains is expressed, but *when* as well. As we approach man on the "evolutionary scale" we find that the ability to delay an action for long periods of time help separate him from his more ancient predecessors.

DELAY is the sine qua non *of the newer brain. Inhibition of desires, drives or wishes gives us the ability to choose and to create civilization. However, delay is often translated into a moral prohibition, which has its own set of dangers to BOTH man and woman and to our esteemed civilization.*

PALEO-PSYCHOLOGY

The creative conflict for man thus is the relationship between his various brains, each with its own reality formula, and in some cases each with its own desires, goals and futures. When there are vast differences in reality formulas, there are also communication gaps. The lower brains and the cortex do not communicate as well as some of us believe or wish. Many times the plans of the cortex are sabotaged by the needs and realities of the older brains, and vice-versa. In fact, the amount of intervention the new brain can have on the older one is often quite minimal. Yoga is one of the few ways the Newer brain can control and modulate the Older brains successfully; however Yoga alone does not know of the reverse. It does not in most instances know how to use the creative forces of the Older brain to enhance the New brain. In other words, a simple world of Yogins would probably not lead to high tech or high art which are creations of New brain interactions. Control and Delay as we know them are not enough for creative brain function. Vitality is also required.

All values are the expression of the reality tunnels of each of the brains. The reptile brain has the "value" of paranoia, suspiciousness, and crude survival. The mammalian brain has more of the same but in a softer, more flexible "furry" fashion. The left brain has the "value" of science, order, logic and control. And the right brain serves art, creativity, invention and insight.

Every culture, every time and every person can be classified according to the value placed on each of these brains. History moves through the phases of each of these brains, and the rise and fall of civilization does the same. We can see the fall of a culture when the left brain attempts to dominate and destroy the needs and desires of the others. We can see the destruction of individuals when, say, the right brain runs the show, or the limbic system is in complete control. *However, it is very important to remember that certain individuals are born with certain brain preferences. Some individuals have fundamental "hard wired" reality tunnels which are solely determined by genetics and early imprinting, and then enhanced or reduced through learning.*

The new brain's ability to inhibit certain older brain functions allows civilization to evolve. However, if these lower functions are "condemned" by the functions of the cortex as in the Middle Eastern Religions of Judaism, Christianity and Islam, we have a revolt. The older brain begins to act out. Think of it as a pressure cooker, which needs to blow off steam but doesn't have a pressure relief valve. It will explode or burn itself out.

"Contempt" of the older brains is similar to a wealthy man having secret disgust for his peasant past.

The Christian religion exemplifies this contempt by its repressive attitudes toward body, instinct and women. Where it dominates the culture is severely split. On the one hand are so-called High Values of love and altruism. On the other hand there is excessive pre-occupation with self, materialism and compulsive sexuality.

The great atrocities associated with Christian civilization are *NOT* caused by the older brains, as they would like us to believe, *BUT* by the New Brain's contempt for its ancestors. The fragility of Christian "ideals" is shown when one culture invades another and considers its enemy to be *NON-HUMAN*. The enemy population are not "people" but embodiments of "Evil." However, the primary "Evil" for the

Christian Religion is *MAN HIMSELF. In practice this means first the body and in particular the woman's body.*

Man is and always has been his own Scapegoat. This can only happen if Man Splits himself into pieces in his efforts to improve herself by acts of transcendence. For this to cease the acts of transcendence must lose their moralistic hateful tone.

Man is not at fault (evil) for splitting himself apart. Our evolution is designed this way. You see, we are a gigantic experiment with unknown futures. The problem here is the cortex's understanding of the whole self is simply limited AND BIASED. The cortex like each of the other brains is self-serving and LIMITED by its genetic, imprinted and LEARNED reality-tunnels.

The cortex attempts to provide pictures of the world which are complete, but in fact are always shallow and fragmented. The ONLY thing equal to the universe is the universe: our brain-pictures (maps and models) are *simplifications* and, usually, *OVER-SIMPLIFICATIONS.*

The cortex "doesn't like" the older brains because their reality sets frequently disturb its desire to have control over the body and nature. The cortex wants power over everything. This sense of self dislikes having its plans and dreams interfered with. When frustrated it looks for *causes* which is almost the same word as *blame* when coupled with Judeo-Christian morality. The cause is always that somebody is a no good shit and should be punished and destroyed. This releases tension and allows the cortex to go on with its delusions of perfect order.

The image of Christ as perfect man is the image of man operating only with his heart. Those who have studied Chakras know that there is more than just the Heart, as psychologists know that there is more than just a cortex. The creation of these partial Gods is a result of projecting either "ideals" or inner powers or both. This appears to result from man's temporary inability to accept all of his functioning brains without worshipping some and despising others. Remember the cortex dislikes the Unknown (Chaos), but the Unknown is both the Mother and the Child of the future.

TANTRA OPENS THE DOOR OF COMMUNICATION

The practice of Western Tantra includes the use and operation of all the brains. In ordinary sex we have the faulty operation of the older brain, contaminated by the repressive fears of the cortex, or the bursting outward of the whole inhibited brain into promiscuity, rape and violence.

Both paths are incomplete and offend either some or all of the brains in question. This frequently leads to further futile attempts to control or destroy.

Western Tantra allows proper benevolent control while at the same time allowing complete gratification. Additionally, the cortex is flooded with the joy and power of the lower brain, again, in a benevolent and respectful fashion.

A significant learning occurs in the areas of love, devotion and visualization, making life rich and elegant.

The practice of Western Tantra is the most sophisticated form of Loving, the most enduring and the most meaningful. It doesn't cut man off from himself, sacrificing one part for the other.

Instead it opens vast channels of communication. The brains grow together, learning to trust each other. Through trust, the brains provide gifts of unimaginable power and joy, something which most of us desire but have no idea of *how* to obtain except through exploitation.

Western Tantra is non-exploitive, yet full of power and satisfaction.

The only drawback of Western Tantra is that it requires a great deal of work. Fortunately, in this case the work is also play.

CHAPTER FOUR

THE ORDER OF
THE WHITE LION

*For I am divided for love's sake, for the chance of union.
This is the creation of the world, that the pain of division
is as nothing and the joy of dissolution all.*
— Liber Al (The Book of the Law)

GODDESS EXPERIENCE ONE

The essence of the story of the emergence of The Order of the
White Lion[1] was revealed to me in 1965 by an elderly woman
(from the South) who claimed to be an adept of an ancient
secret order which somehow linked with the Hermetic Order
of the Golden Dawn.

---

[1] The Order of the White Lion has nothing to do with any rock group
which uses the name to represent itself or its music. In fact the Heads of
the Order, if they existed, would be horrified at this possibility as the
Order doesn't concern itself with the fantasies of Instant Titty. (The
Instant Titty represents a '60s fantasy, first created by Dr. Benjamin
Spock. It demands instant gratification as well as no competition, no
frustration and no struggle for life. It evolved into notions of mystical
equality where all individual differences would be summed and a
golden mean achieved. This concept is best represented by early
communism, and is clandestinely embraced in the Christian West.
However, it is important to remember that while Instant Titty was a
counter proposal to male authoritarianism, it is still a symbol of the
Patriarchy.) The products of Instant Titty can be seen in groups like the
Yuppies. They are elegant consumers waiting to be fed, just because
they are HERE.

I worked with her for approximately nine months at which time I lost contact with her. Her personal hand-made Tarot deck had a White Lion on the Strength card which made a very strong impression on me. She told me that the symbol of the White Lion had major significance for me as well as for the future of mankind.

GODDESS EXPERIENCE TWO

"Tao produced Unity, Unity produced Duality,
Duality produced Trinity, and Trinity
produced all existing things."

"The Ain Soph produced Kether,
from Kether sprang Wisdom and Understanding
and from them all other things appeared."

One Year Later: It was late and I had laid down to rest. My mind wandered over the matters of the day; my classes at the University, my future goals, and my frustrated sex life.

I turned on my back and stared at the ceiling. I put out the joint I was smoking and turned on to my belly. I slowly began rubbing my penis against the soft sheets.

My mind began to struggle as sleep fought for control. All of a sudden I felt a strange sensation near the bottom of my spine. I was preparing to stretch or get up as it was slightly annoying, when I was overwhelmed by a creeping, intense sensation moving up my spinal area. As it reached the nape of my neck there was a momentary blockage, and then finally an explosion of white light inside my head. Almost simultaneously I saw a three dimensional image of Christ on a gigantic cross. He was in grey darkness, as if clouds of rain surrounded Him. There was a Nun dressed in her habit on His right side on her knees (who was removing a watch from His right arm. He did not struggle or resist her, but simply observed what she was doing. He had an empathic, kindly look in His eyes. It seemed as if He was saying Good-Bye.

When the vision ended I experienced the greatest calm and peace I had known. I tried to understand what happened, but couldn't stay awake. I fell into a deep sleep.

Not only was this Kundalini type experience a surprise, but the vision was even more shocking, since I was raised as a Jew, and had adopted a Taoist-Buddhist orientation as an adult. On awakening I thought about the vision for a few moments and began my daily obligations.

I was haunted by this vision from time to time over the years until I realized that one important part of its meaning was that "Time Was Up."

What "time" was the vision communicating? First the time was up for Christ as a western God-head and a carrier of the image of Self. The notion of the suffering male God was coming to an end. The idea that the human race was designed to function as a slave race for God and His Son was ending.

What was emerging was the Goddess, someone who had served the Male God, but now was accepting the mantle of power symbolized by Time and the Watch itself. The watch is frequently used as a symbol of adulthood for males who are about to be *bar mitzvah'd* or married. Second, the notion of Time itself is a powerful invention of the human mind, having great effect on how a race or culture perceives itself. There are notions of circular time, linear time, periodic time, etc. The Christian notion of time is itself epoch based, with clear divisions of stages and events leading to Christ's return and mastery of the world. In my vision Christ lost His watch, His way of knowing what time it was. Instead the Nun, His servant, took the watch. She now was the Time Keeper, and since she did not put the watch on in my vision but held it, this indicates to me that the notion of Time itself would change with the Watch Guard of the Universe.

As many of us are aware, a Changing of The Guard — The Ruling God(dess) — has been taking place for some time and is accelerating. The notion of a Male Master and Female Slave is also changing with equal rapidity.

The reader will understand this section better after reading Norman O. Brown's *Closing Time* or looking at some of Salvador Dali's paintings of melting clocks.

THE UNREDEEMED VIRGIN

The notion of the unredeemed Virgin giving birth to the Son of
the Father so mankind can be redeemed has a certain reso-
nance with Male dominance. Why is the Son redeemed and
the Virgin left unredeemed? Part of the answer lies in Western
man's rejection of his Unconscious and his emotional-animal
nature. The reader must be reminded that the Son and the
Daughter are *co-equals*.

Western psychology and religion, while acknowledging the
Unconscious and the Virgin, place her second to the Son
("every father wants a son"), The Virgin is body and emotion
and the Son is Consciousness, and Reason (the Idol of the
Middle Class).

According to Kabbalistic theory, when the Son and the
Daughter marry, they alchemically are transformed into the
Mother (Binah-Understanding) and the Father (Chokmah-
Wisdom). When this Union is finalized the pair are no longer
separate and are absorbed back into Kether, the Undifferenti-
ated Monad, or Sahasrara, the lotus of a thousand petals.
However, Kether is a word which refers to something which
can not be known by reason, and is only found by experience.
It is the first Point. Something beyond this point is called Ain,
Ain Soph, Ain Soph Aur, or simply Nuit. These terms are
used to imply something beyond Kether, something like
Infinite Space. This sense of infinity is frequently referred to
with such Images as the sleeping, breathing Brahman, the
dark blue Nuit, or the Tao.

Thus, while my vision implied the changing of the Guard
from the Male Christ to the Female Nun, I believe that more
was implied. The "lowly servant" is not adequate on her own
to carry the Watch, the Time of Man and Goddesses.

What is required is a new marriage — not, however,
between a Christly image of blood and misery, the Son of an
angry and jealous God, but between something more noble,
something which reflects the higher and more refined quality
of man, when both Reason and the Unconscious are at last
united, and merged with the *Higher Self* as *Co-Partners*. It
seems that only *Co-Partners* each serving and expressing the

Will of the Self in their own way can heal and forgive Christ and His Consort for their "Sins." More on this in a moment.

As the reader gets into the meat of this book she will find that the sexuality called for is that of the Triplicate: Son-Daughter-God, Mother-Father-Goddess. It is the sexuality of transcendence with neither loss of the "lower" nor negation of the "higher." It is sexuality based on co-equals. It is sexuality founded on bliss, consciousness and intention.

CHRIST & THE LITTLE GIRL

Another insight into my vision is to suggest that it is incomplete. Christ appeared enormous on His Cross. The Nun was on her knees and normal in size. The disparity is obvious, however, it suggests that when one is larger than life more is expected. Have Christ and His Father fallen down on the job? Have they shown their "human-ness" by their failure to care for Man? Has God Himself crushed His own Watch? The association I get from this is that Christ must not pull the Female up to His Stature, nor must the Female pull Him down to Hers. What must be done is that Christ must get off his Cross and She must go toward His Cross. Only by this mutual meeting can the New Aeon be brought in. (Dr. Spiegelman has written an interesting story on this topic, in *Catholicism and Jungian Psychology*, Falcon Press, 1988.)

Typically in our culture the woman's movement has tried to pull man "down" in the process of pulling woman up; and the males who are pro-Goddess have attempted to force the female "up" to male stature. Both attitudes are in error. The best help a male can give the budding Goddess is to move toward her with an open hand, and the best move for the Goddess is to get up off her own knees and move toward him. Sometimes a push in either direction is necessary but that should be enough. If help is too lop-sided for too long, the goal of Co-Equals with the GOD(DESS) as the third is not accomplished. The implication here is that all projections are withdrawn consciously and mutual work begins with the vision set on a shared ideal. Thus the Father is freed to heal Himself and His Daughter is freed from the projection that only His approval will validate Her. He no longer has to throw tantrums because He failed His own projection, and She no longer has to cry, as She knows that His rage simply conveys the pain of His own impotency.

This idea is similar to the principle of the Hexagram — an ancient Hindu symbol of Tantra, which reverses the meaning of the two triangles making up the Hebrew Hexagram sometimes called the Star of David. The "lower" Triangle of the Hexagram the female principle, reaches up, and the "higher" Triangle, the male principle reaches down. Their mutual desire is Union, and each must be willing to leave something behind for the sake of that Union. Each must give up an aspect of personal power, authority and helplessness for the Divine Marriage to take place. The fact that in this interpretation God is Reaching "Down" and His Bride is Reaching "Up" still contains certain aspects of Male dominance. However, the God of this Aeon, particularly in the West is Male; thus He has been in the superior position. He is now aware that this position has to be voluntarily surrendered, and is making His move. The Female on the other hand is surrendering Her "lower" position as well — both for the sake of Union.

Aspects of this model are similar to the psycho-spiritual helping relationship and the parent-child relationship.

The therapist at the right time must leave his chair willingly, without being dethroned by the patient. The patient must leave her chair willingly without being pulled out by the therapist. Without this willingness and effort on both parts the results are incomplete, much like my vision.

THE THIRD GODDESS EXPERIENCE

The Gods Themselves Are Merely Constructs
Out Of Her Maternal Substance.
— Attributed to the God Vishnu, one of the
first Son's Of Man who finally adopted
Mother Kali as His object of worship

Late in 1970 I met and began to work with the Western Mage, Dr. Francis Israel Regardie. During our work together, he taught me certain "exercises" which he modified from the work of Dr. Wilhelm Reich.

Reich and Regardie had communicated a number of times regarding "patients." Although Reich had no use for magick, mysticism or religion, Dr. Regardie found it puzzling that certain aspects of Dr. Reich's therapy were similar to esoteric Yoga practices and in a strange sort of way broke the body down into segments similar to the Chakras of the Hindus. The purpose of Reich's therapy was to help the patient reach "orgastic potency" a sort of whole mind/body orgasm. Reich differentiated this from ejaculatory potency, or the simple ability to have orgasm. He believed that orgastic potency was the norm and civilization bred "it" out of man. He embraced Freud's original definition of "actual neurosis" as energy blockage due to sexual frustration. For Reich, however, sexual frustration was the inability to be orgastically potent. Thus in his therapy, a combination of verbal character analysis and body "work" was designed to help the "neurotic" reach orgastic potency and become truly "normal."

Reich also believed in a universal energy he called "Orgone". He attempted to demonstrate its existence scientifically, but in my opinion failed at this. He explained the world's refusal to accept his theory as resulting from post-Christian humanity's pathological defense (armoring) against the FEAR which orgastic potency evoked.

Reich had great contempt for mysticism, religion, etc., and felt that they only existed because man could not reach full orgasm.

He also had certain notions of a bonding with the Universe, although this was discussed and often disguised through the notion of Orgone. This idea, in one way, became his substitute for the Mystical experience, and possibly for Kundalini.

Many Hindus believe Kundalini is linked with a form of Universal energy, and with the sexual response. The techniques Reich employed and his method for discussing and treating patients held certain similarities to Regardie's and to my Chakra therapy. All of this is not to say that Reich borrowed from the Eastern Yogis and Hinduism; however, Dr. Regardie was fascinated by the similarities. Regardie felt that if an integration between certain methods and ideas suggested by Reich and Kundalini Yoga could be made, a new Tantra, a new Goddess "religion" would begin to emerge in the West.

In fact, Regardie was so fascinated by this idea that at one time he traveled to the East Coast to work on a particular problem with a Kundalini Master. However, as fate would have it, when Regardie arrived he learned that the Master had just died in the crash of a private plane.

It was not until I met Regardie that he again began to entertain this idea consciously. He felt that Reich was on the right track, but that he was still possessed by the patriarchal system and its ideations.

Regardie modified many of Reich's methods to the point that some of them were completely new inventions of his own. We worked on these methods and others and over the years combined them with certain magickal practices as well as Kundalini techniques.

The reader may ask, what are the Goddess qualities to this story? My answer is that both Dr. Reich and Regardie worked with the body and with primordial energies.

In Kabbalah the body, Malkuth, is the Unredeemed Virgin Bride of the Son, the rejected part of the Triplicity.

Both Reich and Regardie, while suffering from their own blindspots, were serving the New Aeon by focusing their attention on the rejected parts of humankind — the body, the animal, the emotions and sexuality.

THE STORY OF THE WHITE LION

The Universe Is Eternal Love Play

It has been prophesized that the Order of the White Lion (OWL) will emerge sometime prior to 2005. However, it will establish its roots sometime in the late 1980's and early 90's as an offshoot of the Original Order of the Knights Templar. The acronym OWL is no simple coincidence: it relates to Horus, the Hawk Headed God of the emerging Aeon. It also relates to the Goddess since the owl was the emblem of

Athena and was associated with Lilith, Anath and the "Eye-Goddess" of ancient Mesopotamia.

As many know, the Knights Templar were involved with the Saracen fraternity of the Hashish-Takers. One of the original purposes of the Knights (before the Church wrenched them away from the service of the 'Lady' and coerced them to fight for the Church) was to aid and uphold the feminine Goddess, which included the practice of a secret form of Tantra. This spiritual quest was degraded by the Church's attempt to remove the power of the Goddess by making her the mother of God, relegating her to a secondary position. The idea of reducing the female to insignificance can be seen in this quote by a silversmith in Acts 19:26–27: "... this man Paul has persuaded and converted a great number of people with his argument that gods made by hand are not gods at all. This threatens not only to discredit our trade, but also to reduce the sanctuary of the great goddess Diana to unimportance. It could end up by taking away all the prestige of a goddess venerated all over Asia, yes, and everywhere in the civilized world."

The romantic tales of Lancelot, Parsifal, Galahad, etc. also enhanced the image of the helpless female which held great appeal for men and does so even today, particularly in the South. The greatest danger to a budding Goddess is always a gentleman.[1]

---

[1] The idea of slaying the Dragon to rescue the distressed maiden has great psychological import. (The dragon/serpent is an allegory for the Kundalini Force. However, the notion of slaying versus integrating is purely Christian-Judeo.) An important meaning here is that males can only enter the mysteries of the Goddess, once they have faced, conquered and *integrated* the power of their own beast. This is why the Knights were pre-occupied with loyalty and betrayal. Their image, which was often portrayed as kind and holy, was frequently tarnished by deception, lust and greed. In other words, they required the image of the helpless female as a device to rescue themselves from their own feminine attributes.

(KING KONG represents an interesting degeneration of the myth. The hero [Bruce Cabot] cannot slay the Monster [Kong] personally, and airplanes — images of our technological-military civilization —

The Christian Church was instrumental in projecting all negative qualities on the female.[1] Augustine and other Church Fathers believed that only a Male born from the Father could defeat death and redeem the beast in man. The female became the scapegoat for the male's inability to integrate and cope with his own darkness, his own beast within. The world which Jesus was later to judge was seen as the bestial body of the female which the early Church openly loathed.

In the Christian world, darkness takes away from the image of God, rather than "adding" to it and, as such, its existence must be accounted for by division and isolation.

The Lion was often a symbol associated with images of the Great Goddess, such as Astarte, Cybele, Ishtar and Hathor, all of whom rode or drove lions and often appeared in the form of a lioness or lion-headed female. Her many names have been associated with both Power and the practice of Tantra. (Look at the Strength Card in the Tarot. Why does it appear that a female is controlling the Jaws of the Lion?)

The Goddesses of the Lion were law givers, creators of cities, the mothers of both the Gods and men, the fierce destroyers of obsolete civilizations and the human race. It has been noted that in a conversation with Ra, She replied to his request to stop slaying mankind by saying, "When I slay men my heart rejoices.". However, through Her grace man was also allowed to learn about the nature of the Gods.[2]

---

do the job for him. Modern man does not see himself as Hero, but sees his weapons and tools as Gods. One of the purposes of OWL is to reverse this process.)

[1] Image making is always interesting, as it requires rejecting certain qualities, while emphasizing others. Males have the awful tendency of projecting all traits and tendencies which are regarded as inferior or negative onto females as a result of the sex-differentiated socialization process engendered by the Patriarchal system.

[2] The image of the Goddess as both the nurturing Mother and the destroyer and devourer of her own children is disturbing to the Christian "Mind," but long recognized as an essential Wisdom in the East. It represents the acknowledgment of the opposites on the Tree of Life, and begins to imply the Middle Pillar of Mildness.

The West borrowed her power and force and of course attributed it to such images as King Richard the Lion Hearted, King Arthur and many others.

The symbol of White as used here must not be associated with ideas of Christian purity and virginity. White originally had nothing to do with such infantile and hysterical fantasies. The best I can make of the idea of White is that it represents an idea which is difficult to convey by words and concepts. White light is undifferentiated. It is the origin, as the Tree of Life intimates, of the completely unknowable qualities of Nuit — "Infinite Space and the Infinite Stars thereof" — manifested in Kether, the highest light on the Tree, the first point of reference with which man can even begin to cope.

The development of OWL as a living Order will emerge after the major thrust of the feminist movement "failed." The original Women's Liberation movement was supposed to be the basis of the re-emergence of the feminine as a powerful force in the universe; however it was deeply contaminated by the puritanical and cantankerous influence of the Male Gods, no doubt a contributing factor in its failure.

First, the psychology of the patriarchal identification of the feminine has to be altered. This means that the feminine can not find its true roots by imitating western patriarchal consciousness. As many will note, what woman wanted she didn't get. The stone tablets of Moses cracked just enough to encircle her in the charms and trappings of the paternal system.

The purpose of the Order of the White Lion will be to help usher in the New Aeon by establishing a group of leaders and supporters who will help the Goddess emerge in totally unexpected ways. (In fact do not be surprised or shocked if women lose "rights" before they gain the power to define their rights.)

The Order will establish fellowships of older males and females (brothers and sisters) which will be concerned with practicing the ancient arts. More importantly it will be involved in training younger females as Scientists, Inventors, and Artists, who through their creative genius will help replace the arthritic patriarchy as painlessly as nature will allow.

These new women will come from all classes. Each will have exceptional intelligence. The purpose of the Order will be to save as many of them and their children as possible from being absorbed into the reproduction bias, wild man-hating, or the patriarchal prison of glitter.

Those that are the most able will be trained in ancient and modern thinking, science, and art. They will be taught to respect and revere their own sexuality in a new and most revealing way.

Training will be vigorous and only the best suited for the task will complete the entire course.

The above myth of such an Order is an ancient one; however, it is only now in the latter part of the 20th century, that women have enough apparent freedom to undertake such a difficult and profound journey.[1]

---

[1] As the reader will observe, the OWL is not a Christian Order, nor was the Golden Dawn. One attribute among many others of the Golden Dawn which gives the whole show away is the equality between male and female adepts. The practice of Tantra was never directly mentioned in classic Golden Dawn texts although there are numerous sex-negative references. This is due to the fact that the original teachings fell into the hands of the Christians as well into other hands who disguised its real meaning to protect it from the jealous and dangerous Church. The new Golden Dawn which is now emerging no longer has to disguise its real purposes or its association with the Knights Templar, the Illuminati and other Tantric groups.

To this day I am amazed by how many people believe that the Golden Dawn is a Christian Order, and that Dr. Regardie supported the Christian value system. I am even more amazed that individuals think that I support the idea of Christianity in any form. I still have a few disciples who are deluding themselves by interpreting what I say as being a form of Christian mysticism.

The reverse of this is also false, and equally amusing. Many people believe that the Golden Dawn is an offshoot of Satanism and that Dr. Regardie and I are Satanists.

The Golden Dawn is a development of the Rosicrucian Order (mystics who called themselves Knights of the Rosy Cross) who borrowed the symbols and colors of earlier pagan groups, mystical

Of course much UNDOING will be necessary to prepare the new Goddess, and much of it will be done by middle age and older males, and by those females who have had more experience with the patriarchal deceits, lies and paraphernalia. Some of these males may at present be considered "failures" themselves, but in the new Aeon they will utilize what they learned about the true nature of the system.

JAMES BOND & THE ELITIST FEMALE

We find the elitist female myth exploited in numerous James Bond stories, where superior women are both adversaries and helpers of Bond. As usual, they submit to his superior male powers and thus fall from their throne. In other words, it was the female's devotional quality which was exploited and which caused her to fall and become the slave of man. This is intentional since loving loyalty is the quality that the patriarchy most fears about women. Why might this be? One of the worst threats to any patriarchal system occurs when competency and power are joined with commitment and loyalty. With these "virtues" alone empires have toppled.

Ian Fleming was no fool however, since he did have the vision which brought to mass consciousness the strength and power of the female life force.

BEYOND MATRIARCHY

The Order of the White Lion will have more in mind than to simply return to a Matriarchal view of the Universe. Its goal is the transcendence of the sex differences as we know them. The secret meaning behind this is now being revealed in subtle and

---

Jews, the Egyptians and the Hindus. These were later transformed into Christian symbols. Remember the Rosicrucian symbol was a White Rose with a Red Cross. During the Crusades the Christians adopted the symbol and said that it was representative of "innocence and blood" when in fact it was the emblem of the "Assassins" (a mispronunciation of the Saracenic brotherhood of hashishim, the "hashish-takers"), the forerunner of the Knights Templar. The Rose represented the female anatomy and the Cross, the male.

various ways and may be enhanced by the practices presented in the Tantric section of this book.

To my knowledge, the Order has not made an overt appearance. Nor do I know of any organizations with the financial base and Will to bring such an Order into existence.

However, I have met many males in recent years who have indirectly and unconsciously supported OWL, although their support has been somewhat masochistic and ignoble and frequently filled with saccharin male hysteria (Christian Ideals and sex-denial mixing with Pagan Lust) and empty clichés. Here again, most of these males, while trying to help the Goddess re-emerge, are terrified of the depths of her Psyche and spend a good deal of time suppressing its manifestations. Some of these types have sought me out. However, once I treat them to the dark side of their own image they promptly cast me in the role of devil and continue on in their hysterical ways. From time to time a few try to hold on but generally their fear prevents them from doing any real work.

In addition to working with the Feminine Force, the Order is to work with rejected children in a way never before attempted on this planet. Rather than helping them live boring and hum-drum lives they will be taught to live superior lives. Again, to my knowledge, this has not yet been achieved or even advertised.

Once the Order has planted its seed it will disappear, as it will be of no further use. This will happen sometime between 2090 and 2150.

This entire scenario is based on the assumption that the Western World will experience numerous, great upheavals. While I do not suffer from *geographomania,* I have it on good report that the OWL will first manifest itself in the English speaking world.

(The OWL, incidentally, is the traditional symbol of Athene, Goddess of strategy and tactics.)

Another bizarre teaching of the Order is that *WE ARE ALL ALIENS.*

All of history as reflected in our ethical philosophies, religions and secret orders are bastardized accounts containing one message — *Transcendence.*

What transcendence means is nothing more than focusing on our *alien* qualities, while de-focusing on our *earthly* qualities. Unfortunately, the way that this has been taught has been both foolish and destructive. The Gnostics and Manicheans, for instance, rejected Earth but forgot our ALIEN heritage. They gradually rejected the whole Universe ... and the Christians copied them.

The secret of Transcendence is not negation nor is it affirmation. It is simply an act of *POWER Concentration* without placing a moral value on what is transcended.

Restated simply, it does not matter whether you transcend eating habits, sexual habits, drug habits, clothes habits, or the way you open a door. What matters is that you *transcend* — pause before reacting mechanically — and by repetitive *acts* of transcendence, consciousness becomes transformed. You can see why indulgence as a hedonic notion, and abstinence as a Christian notion, and compulsion as a Psychological notion, have no place in Transcendence, except as *Technique.*

Additionally, transcendence cannot be reduced to secret messages from the Psyche, secret orders, drug related experiences etc. It demands *WORK.*

Everything else is simply information, the lowest form of knowledge. Without transcendence permeating the Ego and the Psyche, very little will be accomplished.

In other words, it is time to stop talking about Gods, messages, channels, etc. and time to act like the Gods/Goddesses we *are.* It is time to stop waiting and wondering and it is time to start acting and doing.

Incidentally the proof that we are aliens is very simple. There is nothing like us upon the planet earth — nothing at all.

We are the definers of what we can be. This is the difference between Joe Smith and Rover, his dog. Rover cannot *change itself at will* into something different. Joe can. We Aliens can even transcend the habit of death and stupidity if we put our efforts into it.

Only transcendence — DELAY combined with WILL — can lead to more transcendence. We can get out of our mess by doing something different. The first act is to realize that we are, in fact, *Aliens*.

The next step is to *practice being Alien all day long*.

This is accomplished by using your imagination, *dis*-identifying with your conflicts and by *doing*. Don't *Re-Act* mechanically like an animal. *Act* creatively, like an alien.

What if the Order as revealed to me is only fiction and the whim of an old woman's mind, supported by myself and others for our own need to manifest our True Will?

There is no way to answer the question of legitimacy. The Catholic Church had a nightmare and made it come true. So, does that prove the legitimacy of the Catholic nightmare? I do not think so. What it does prove is that validity cannot be proven by simple existence over time. Hitler's nightmare came true also.

What we do know is that if the potential is there and if enough *power* and *force* is placed behind that potential then almost anything can come true. This method has little or nothing to do with our primitive notions of morality, belief or faith. What it does prove is that power *works*. The future exists first in Fantasy, then in Will, and finally, in Reality.

The Tantric methods and techniques which follow were not given to me by the old lady referred to above. It was worked out from my own visions and the work I did with many individuals. Particularly important is the time I spent with my teacher, Dr. Francis Israel Regardie to whom I dedicate this work.

CHAPTER FIVE

DEVOTIONAL SEXUALITY
IT TAKES THREE TO MAKE ONE

The practice of Tantra, whether Eastern or Western, is associated with the GREAT GODDESS.

Western Tantra focuses on releasing Kundalini. It uses the Tarot, the symbols of the Tree of Life, Bio-energetic techniques and the Chakras to help aspirants obtain the pure essence of both Magick (Power) and Mysticism (Love).

Note: Magick and Mysticism (or Power and Love) are *constructs* which embrace a false dichotomy which has been perpetrated by the Christian ethos. This philosophy teaches that *power* (activity and self-related pursuits) are *necessarily evil*, while *love* (passivity and other-related interests) are *necessarily good*. This slavish philosophy, whose aim is to turn all men into sheep, is identified with God as "Good Shepherd"; but its emphasis is placed on the act of *pleading* as the fundamental form of worship and stands in stark contrast to the practices of Magic and Meditation which are based on Action and Will. Great Love is Great Power and Great Power is Great Love. Any force taken to its ultimate transmutes itself into the All.

THE TREE OF LIFE SYMBOLS

The Tree of Life, a creation of the Kabbalists, is one of many useful models for gaining insight and intuitive awareness of how Tantra works. It was from my work with the Tree of Life and Sexual Magick that this system evolved and so I have a special place in my heart for this model. However, if you find this model difficult or cumbersome, feel free to use the Eastern model for meditation and association. Better yet, use both. (The reader who is unfamiliar with the Tree of Life is referred to the appendix of this book.)

THE FORMULA

Kether is the Point, or Crown.

Chokmah is the Father Principle.

Connecting the two is a straight line, which being one-dimensional cannot encompass space.

Adding Binah, the Great Productive Mother, a Triangle is created which metaphorically encompasses space. This "lower" triangle with the point yearning for "heaven" is the symbol of the female force which is said to govern the earth, while desiring union with "higher" forces. The triangle pointed downward is the male force yearning for union with the female force. (Note: In the Tantric hexagram the downward pointing triangle represents the female or Yoni and the upward pointing triangle, the male Lingam.) When the triangles meet as they do in the so-called Star of David, we have Union of the two forces. The six rayed star was first a symbol of ancient Tantra before it became a symbol of the Jewish people. Interestingly enough, the lower Triangle can be seen as the Shekinah (the female counterpart of Jehovah), and the upper Triangle can be seen as Jehovah. Each are yearning for Union which symbolically takes place on the Jewish Sabbath.

Another important aspect of this symbol is that when the two triangles join, a hexagram is formed that has a seventh point which is in the center of both. This is referred to as the Heart of Union, where the male and female energies mix and coalesce with the forces of the Goddess.

In Tantra, each act always includes the emanating force of Kether, the Crown of the Tree of Life. Therefore in the practice of Western Tantra, a God-form is always included, bringing the participants to Three — the man, the woman and the Deity. Thus in Tantra we can say that the relationship is not only *governed* by the Goddess but also *includes* Her.

Unlike ordinary relationships, those which include the God-Form possess a transcendental quality of Love and Power.

This is hinted at by the triangle symbol found in traditions as opposite as Catholicism and Masonry and as diverse as Taoism and Egyptian Magick. In the Tantric tradition the triangle represents the Kali Yantra or Primordial Image — the Triangle of Life. According to oriental sages, "The object of the worship of the Yantra is to attain unity with the Mother of the Universe in Her forms as Mind, Life and Matter ..."

As we descend the Tree from Kether, the Monad, to Chokmah, the Father, we find that Binah, the Great Mother Principle is the Third point of emanation. The new energy brought into the relationship is neither the Father nor the Mother but Kether. This is the essential point of energy which is either forgotten or never employed in the ordinary act of sexual intercourse.

The process of Tantric intercourse is symbolized by *WHITE LIGHT*. Once again, I cannot adequately emphasize that the precepts of Christian morality have nothing to do with the phenomena of *WHITE LIGHT*. You would do better to think of it as an Atom Bomb, or LSD, hitting your brain with a stick.

Although Kether is the first Sephiroth on the Kabbalistic Tree of Life, for the sake of reference in the practice of Tantra we include it as the third symbolic participant in the act. This concept is introduced and included here, since God-Forms are typically left out of ordinary sexual practices.

As to the subject of "Occult Eugenics", a statement of its importance is proper here. Essentially, this study and practice concerns itself with the creation proper of the Magickal Child. This is rarely practiced, of course, as is evidenced by the paucity of real "Magicians" as well as true genius, great art, intentional work, etc.

The practice of Western Tantra brings the energy up from Malkuth to Kether. As you develop your practice, you bring Kether back down to Malkuth, finally "mixing" both in Tiphareth. This form of Intercourse is intentional and conscious. Unlike its ordinary counterpart, Tantric Intercourse creates a different type of energy which "feeds" the Universe.

Noting the Tree again, the Son of the Parents, Chokmah and Binah, when filled with the power of Kether, is Tiphareth. The daughter is Malkuth. Of course this is *symbolic,* simply a model to convey a deeper truth. In addition to the forces previously mentioned the powers of the other Sephira must be generated to create the desired effects.

Tiphareth is frequently associated with the Heart Chakra. Malkuth is viewed as the Bride of Kether, manifested in the world; her purity is the result of Chokmah and Binah combining with Kether. Thus the well-known Kabbalistic verse, "Malkuth is in Kether, and Kether is in Malkuth, albeit different in kind." (With reference to the Tarot then, we see that the Path between Kether, [the Crown], and Tiphareth, [the Heart Chakra] is guarded by the High Priestess.)

The High Priestess guards the mysteries and is both the destroyer and creator of those who cross the Abyss.

The practice of Occult Eugenics whether for the purpose of *creating a living physical entity, or a spiritual God-form*, functions by combining the energy of Kether and Malkuth. In concrete terms, we bring the force up, and we bring the force down, mixing them at the point of Tiphareth, the center of the Tree of Life, whose correlate within the physical body is the region of the Heart.

As the practitioner will discover, the correct practice of Western Tantra (Sexual Ecology) assures that the God-forms we create will act according to the power and essence used to generate them. (Later I will describe the use of the Tarot symbols to define the force you wish to create.)

CHAPTER SIX

PREPARING FOR ORGASM

EXERCISES

THE METHODS PRESENTED HERE WILL CAUSE TREMENDOUS CHANGES IN YOUR SEXUAL AND SPIRITUAL LIFE, AS WELL AS EVERY OTHER ASPECT OF YOUR EXISTENCE. THEREFORE DO NOT UNDERTAKE THESE EXERCISES UNTIL YOU ARE ABSOLUTELY CERTAIN THAT YOU ARE BOTH READY AND WILLING TO CHANGE. REMEMBER: BY ITS VERY NATURE, ALL GENUINE SPIRITUAL CHANGE BRINGS UNPREDICTABLE RESULTS.

BE SURE YOU HAVE BECOME EXPERT AT THE WARM-UP EXERCISES BEFORE YOU ATTEMPT THE MORE COMPLICATED ONES.

PLEASE READ THESE INSTRUCTIONS AT LEAST THREE TIMES, SEPARATED BY AT LEAST ONE DAY. DO NOT PERFORM MORE THAN TWO SESSIONS A WEEK.

As These Movements And Techniques Are Very Powerful,
Please Make Haste Slowly.

The movements described in this chapter are preliminary to any form of Tantric practice, although the simpler forms of pre-Tantric Intercourse may be practiced at the same time. (See Chapter Eight.)

Once these movements have produced their prescribed effect, certain bio-physical events will begin to take place; events which will increase both the depth and breadth of the orgasm, elevating it from its purely emotional and physical base to a higher level. As such, these movements have been specifically designed to aid you in eliminating those negative effects of culturization which have impeded your evolution.

No one is free from psycho/sexual/spiritual contamination, particularly if exposed to Western civilization during the formative years.

I do not care how "free" one seems or how promiscuous one is. Ordinary therapy will not help you, nor will education. There are only a few ways and this method is one of them.

These *essential exercises* are presented in two forms, one are called Method(s) and consist of quick warm-up movements and the second form are called Sections which are the *essential movements.* One of the Warm-Up exercises should be used prior to each essential movement. Alternate Warm-Up methods as you choose, but leave nothing out.

Prior to starting any of these exercises make sure your bladder and bowels are empty and that two hours have passed since your last meal.

Note: The purpose of these exercises is to remove chronic muscle tensions. You will experience "explosions" of energy and some clonisms (tremors or shudders) if you do the exercises properly. Be prepared for this and do not be frightened when it happens.

WARM-UP METHOD ONE

Step 1. Sit, lie down or stand up. Make Faces — Stretch all the muscles in the face. Open your mouth as wide as you can, move the jaw from side to side. At the same time open your eyes as wide as you can. Move your eyes up and down and from side to side. This will begin to release tension, thereby removing obsessive thoughts which lie hidden in these areas. Make many different faces. Use a mirror if you wish. Do this for 5 minutes.

Step 2. Hum and chatter — Hum from the depths of your belly. Use Om or just Um. Do this for one to two minutes. Now stick your tongue out and chatter DADA, MAMA, BABA. Stick out your jaw as far as you can and continue humming and chattering. Do this for 3 minutes.

Step 3. Pull your shoulders up as if you were trying to reach your ears. Hold for several seconds feeling the strain then drop them as low as you can. Repeat this for 2 minutes.

Step 4. With your mouth open take in a deep breath inflating your chest and pulling your stomach in and up. Hold for a count of 5 and then just let the chest fall and the belly relax. Repeat this 10 times allowing a count of 7 to elapse before your next inhalation.

Step 5. Turn your head from side to side as slowly and as far as you can. Repeat for 1 minute.

Step 6. Lying down on your back, hold your legs about 4 inches off the ground and stretch arms and legs outward. Hold this as long as you can then let them drop. Repeat 2 times.

Step 7. With your mouth slightly open breathe rapidly, sighing as you exhale. Continue for 2 minutes.

WARM-UP METHOD TWO

Lie down on your back. Take ten to 15 deep breaths starting deep in your belly and working it upward. Try to become aware of all the muscles you use in breathing. When you have completed this, slowly get up. Stand with your feet slightly apart and count to three. When you reach three let the top part of your body collapse forward and downward at your waist, like a rag doll. Do not fall, just let it collapse; do not force it, let gravity pull it down. Repeat this 10 times. When you are finished take a few deep breaths and feel the effect this exercise had on you. See if you can sense your pelvic region. Now repeat the same experiment this time exhaling rapidly through your mouth as you fall and breathing in slowly as you rise. Repeat this 10 times.

WARM-UP METHOD THREE

Stand up with your feet slightly apart and bend your knees slightly (not too much) and then let the top part of your body flop forward. Do not force it — just let it drop.

While in this position, use a five count breath (through your mouth). Five in, hold five, five out, hold five. Repeat this three times and slowly straighten yourself up. Repeat this 5 times.

Now, stand erect for a few moments with your eyes tightly shut. Become aware of any tension in your face, neck or shoulders. Mobilize these tensions by opening your mouth as wide as you can and distorting your face. Now close your mouth and continue on with the distortions. When you've done this for at least 3 minutes, tilt your head back as far as you can, and begin turning it very slowly from side to side. Some people might get nauseous at this point, so be prepared. If you experience the urge to vomit go right ahead, since the gag reflex is marvelous for reducing deep body tension.

SECTION ONE

The Essential Movements

Remove your clothes, or wear loose fitting clothing.

Lie down on a very soft surface in a cool room. If your room is too warm turn up the air conditioning slightly, or turn on a fan. *Coolness is very important.*

Stretch thoroughly. Move your arms to your side and take a deep breath. Hold your breath, while doing a slow, controlled sit up. Let the breath go and flop. Repeat the breath, sit up and flop two or three times. Stretch again.

Get into the "breathing position." This means that you are to lie on your back with your knees bent and your feet solidly on the floor or bed about a foot from your rear end. Your knees should be about 18 inches apart. Your arms should be at your side.

Now begin breathing through your mouth. Make sure your mouth is held *loosely* open, (about 1 inch). Inhale to a slow count of three, then exhale to a slow count of three.

We will call this "deep breathing." The inhalation should be full but NOT forced. Start inhaling from your *lower belly*. The belly should begin to expand first, followed by the chest. *This is essential.*

When the inhalation reaches its highest point, JUST LET GO saying "AH", allowing the chest and belly to collapse/ contract on their own.

Make no voluntary movements as you breathe. If you sense tension leave it alone. Allow what happens to just happen. Remember, allow a slow count of three while inhaling and begin exhaling by saying "AH". You should set a timer for 20 minutes. Then just sense and feel your body for another 5 minutes. Verbalize *only* what you sense and feel. Make no interpretations at this time.

Now you will combine deep breathing with other movements. As you do the following exercises you may at times notice that your breathing becomes erratic or even that you unconsciously hold your breath. *Do not allow this to continue.* It is essential that you continue deep breathing throughout the exercise unless specifically instructed otherwise.

Again start deep breathing for at least five minutes. Continue deep breathing, but now open your eyes as wide as you can while inhaling and then exhale closing your eyes as tight as you can. Utilize just the section of your head from the eyes up. Do not move your jaw or change the position of your body. Do this for 5 minutes.

After you have done this, continue deep breathing but this time lift your head while inhaling and let it flop on the exhalation. (Be sure to have something soft to catch your head.)

Some people get nauseous during this phase, so have an empty stomach or keep a pot handy. Set your timer for 3 minutes. After you feel comfortable you may increase the timer to 10 minutes.

When this phase is completed become totally aware of your sensations and feelings for five minutes or so. Be sure to verbalize what is going on. Again, *no interpretations*.

Next, begin deep breathing again; on the inhalation push your lower jaw out as far as you can. On the exhalation, let it relax. Keep this up for 5 minutes. Allow any automatic grimaces to develop. Become aware of any heat that develops.

Relax for a moment or two. Begin deep breathing again. On the inhalation push your lower jaw out as far as possible, but this time growl like an animal on the exhalation. The growl should be as full and deep as possible. Begin to become aware of the *origin* of your growl. Do not do this exercise for more than *one* minute. When finished, relax for a moment or two.

If you are not already in bed, please lie down now. Lie supine (on your back). I want you to put the two exercises together along with a few other movements.

On the inhalation stick your jaw out as far as you can and at the same time raise your arms *slowly* behind your head. At the same time begin lifting your head toward your chest and growl, leaving your arms behind your head.

When you are almost finished growling and your chin almost touches your chest, clench your fists and fling your arms outward and sideways, hitting the bed. Let go with a yell as your arms hit the bed. Be sure to let your head fall back on the bed.

Repeat this procedure six times.

It is very important to relax now. Give yourself a break. I would suggest at least ten minutes of just plain sensing and feeling.

You may now stop for this session or continue on with Section Two. For beginners, I suggest that you STOP.

SECTION TWO

Begin by lying down and sensing and feeling your body. Do this for at least five minutes. Ten minutes is better.

Now begin deep breathing as described previously. Ten minutes of breathing will do.

Raise your hands straight up in the air over your chest. Inhale, then stretch the left arm and relax the right arm as you exhale. Then inhale, stretch the right arm and relax the left arm as you exhale. Continue alternating arms. Reach for the sky as you say "AH" with every attempt. REACH up as high as you can, as if your greatest desire was just out of reach. To help you get the feeling of this movement you might say the name of a person who you would like to make contact with. Sometimes "Maamee" or "Dadee" can create the desired feeling, or just yell "Give Me!" Learning how to YEARN is very important later to both Tantra work and Devotional prayer. (See my article on Active Prayer in *Healing Energy, Prayer and Relaxation* by Israel Regardie, Falcon Press, 1989.)

Continue with this exercise until your arms begin to get tired. Now, just let go. Relax. (Yes: this is activating the quest for Instant Titty and much more. You have to experience it consciously to transcend it.)

I can't over-emphasize the importance of yearning, both in releasing repressions and to help you learn *devotional sexuality.*

Next, repeat the above movement except this time reach up with both arms at the same time on the exhalation and relax both on the inhalation repeating either the name of a significant other or a Divine name. (See *The Complete Golden Dawn System of Magic,* 1984, Falcon Press, for Divine names; or use **IAO** — pronounced ee – aah – oh — which will serve well for most students.)

Repeat this movement until your arms become very tired. Be sure to reach as high as you can.

Now treat yourself to some fun food such as ice cream, cake or popcorn. If you choose ice cream be conscious of the Melting Sensation.

SECTION THREE

I must again warn the reader at this point that these movements are designed to open up areas of consciousness filled with psycho-spiritual energies. Proceed slowly. Do not lust after results.

This is a good time to discuss journals. If you are serious about your personal work a special journal should be on hand to record the results of your work. This might include feelings, thoughts, dreams, divinations etc. which have occurred after you have begun your practices. This record will be essential if you desire to go further in your Tantric practices.

Lie down and begin deep breathing for 20 minutes.

Begin by opening and closing the eyes as described in section one for another five minutes.

Relax, sense and feel your body for ten minutes.

Now I want you to breath *backwards*. This means on the inhalation pull your belly *in* and pull your chest up making the sound of a wheeze. (This should sound similar to someone who has a very bad chest cold.) Hold the breath for one or two seconds and let your chest collapse. Relax for one minute and repeat the backwards breath 5 times. Relax again and repeat 5 times. Do 6 more sets. You can increase the breathing movements to 10 times as well as increasing the sets to 10 when you become comfortable with this movement.

Relax and treat yourself to some gooey goodie.

SECTION FOUR

Begin deep breathing for 15 minutes. Then as you continue breathing, on the inhalation slowly tilt your pelvis toward your face. On the exhalation let it DROP. Repeat this for 15 minutes. Do not tilt any part of your body except your pelvis.

Now slowly bring your knees together on the inhalation and let them fall open on the exhalation. Continue this for 10 minutes. If your legs, or for that matter anything else, begin to quiver or shake, just allow this to happen. (And by the way, congratulations.)

Now rest for at least 10 minutes, sensing and feeling your body.

Begin breathing again, this time with your legs flat on the bed. On the inhalation lift up your right leg and on the exhalation strike the bed as hard as you can with it. Now do this with the left leg. Alternate legs for 5 minutes. If the circumstances allow, give out a loud shout as your leg strikes the bed.

Relax. Sense and feel your body for at least 15 minutes.

IMPORTANT NOTES

Begin with the movements in Section One and work your way through each section to Section Four. Do *not* begin from Section Four and work your way backward.

Sections One and Two can be practiced together.

Section Three and Four should *not* be practiced together until you feel comfortable with the results of Sections One and Two.

Start a journal and use a tape recorder during your sessions.

No session should be longer than one hour.

If you have medical problems consult your doctor before undertaking the movements.

You will be shaky for at least ten minutes after your sessions. Do not drive or operate dangerous equipment.

After six months of practice you can try a GRAND session of four hours using all the movements in the described sequence.

After a year of practice you can begin to mix up the movements when it suits your needs.

These are bio-psycho-spiritual exercises and only individuals who have chosen the Path toward enlightenment and self-development in the most profound sense should undertake these movements.

These movements can and should be used throughout your entire life. Not only will they help decrease depression and anxiety, they will continue to bring you insight and new energy.

CHAPTER SEVEN

THE PSYCHO-SPIRITUAL MEANING OF THE CHAKRAS

"I have been deluded from birth that I was born head first. Thus it has been my task to discover what direction I really came from and in what direction I shall return." (Hyatt discussing this issue with Israel Regardie, 1983–84.)

Regardie replied: *"In your case you even have a deeper quest. You didn't have to travel at all, they yanked you out of the belly."*

I have decided to employ the marvelous work of J. Marvin Spiegelman, Ph.D., on Kundalini and the Chakras. The reason I have chosen his work is four-fold. First, he is a Zurich trained Jungian analyst and thus is fully qualified to discuss the psychological aspects of Kundalini and the Chakras, which helps give a Western perspective to an Eastern creation.

Second, he, too, worked with the famed Psycho-Spiritual teacher, Dr. Israel Regardie in the area of Neo-Reichian therapy. This makes him uniquely qualified to help the student understand the relationship between "mind and body."

Thirdly, I spent a number of years in Jungian analysis with Dr. Spiegelman and can personally attest to his understanding of these matters.

Finally, we have kept up a relationship for over twenty years in the areas of psychology and mysticism (as well as an abiding personal friendship) and thus I can speak for his dedication and understanding of the topic.

According to Dr. Spiegelman, "The chakras may be defined as 'subtle centers of operation in the body of the Shaktis or Powers of the various Tattvas or Principles' (Avalon). Just as consciousness is not simply a function of the body or its organs however, just so can we not simply describe the chakras as physiological activity. Consciousness is not an organic conception but is itself primary, or antecedent. It is rather more correct to think of the body and its various centers as 'veiled' expressions of consciousness. Indeed, as consciousness goes from the abstract to the subtle to the concrete, we see the increasingly veiled condition of it, so that it can even appear as unconsciousness. Yet all aspects are conditions of consciousness. So, then, when the centers are described, these are seen as in Western physiology, even where this is more detailed than in the latter, and transcending it."

Dr. Spiegelman's comment should in no way be seen as ignoring the body. As he says, "the purification of the body is necessary for the purification of the mind." I, however, do not distinguish between the body, the mind and consciousness, except for reference sake and for effect, by the use of metaphor. The sincere practice of Western Tantra creates the necessary experience which smashes all such illusions of opposites.

Dr. Spiegelman continues in his psychological analysis of chakras: "... Jung expressed it by saying that each chakra is a whole world. One might say that this means that a different type of consciousness is being described for each of them ... When we go more deeply into the symbolism, we will see that whole world-views can be contained in each of them — indeed whole types of religious attitude. It is little wonder, then, that this ancient tradition has been so long-lasting, and has had its impact on others religions as well."

As one studies Dr. Spiegelman's psychological descriptions he will begin to see how the student is transformed from being the automatic food of the gods in the spiritual food chain, to one who deliberately sacrifices himself as he ascends the ladder. In our method of Tantra and Chakra working we also lose our obsessions with "mineness." This is not a moralistic statement which contains the notion that "one should be this or that", but a pragmatic one. Your best interests are not served by greediness nor are they served by elevating yourself because you are not greedy. Living and operating as a blind consumer and object of consumption is limited and stupid.

As our perspective evolves we are neither obsessed with ideas of passion and desire nor are we overwhelmed by them. The normal points of conflict, discussion and moralizing of *homo normalis* are gone, yet they are never forgotten as the roots which have led to our own power of bliss.

DEFINITIONS & PSYCHOLOGICAL ASSOCIATIONS OF THE CHAKRAS

I have taken the position that Sahasrara is not a Chakra in the usual sense of the term. I see it as a bridge from the symbolic head to something beyond. In this sense, it is metaphorical. While specific god-names and images can be applied to it, it is beyond all word definitions and can only be known through experience. In order to provide some sense of continuity with other systems I still assign aspects of Kether (the Crown) to it; however, I also assign the metaphor Ain (Dark-to-Light) as well. I believe that this helps create the feeling of *beyondness*.

The Kabbalistic associations to Hindu Chakras are made for creative and associative purposes. Please do not take them literally, but simply as suggestive. While Dr. Regardie has also agreed from one point of view with the associations I have made, he and others have also used the following:

Kether: Sahasrara Chakra.
Chokmah: Ajna Chakra.
Binah: Vishuddha Chakra.

The "Final" Point Of Transition

Chesed
Geburah : All to Anahata Chakra.
Tiphareth

The First Point Of Transition

Netzach: Svadhisthana Chakra.
Hod: Manipura Chakra.
Yesod: Muladhara Chakra.

Malkuth

As the reader will note, there are still two major divisions or transformational gaps, regardless of which group of associations the student prefers. The significance of these points of transition will become clearer as the reader continues. You will note below that the final transition takes place between Ajna and Sahasrara. The reason for the difference is simple. In the Western Tradition there are three orders; the outer order, the inner order, and finally the Secret Invisible Order. The outer order consists of Malkuth, Yesod, Hod, and Netzach energies. The inner order consists of Tiphareth, Geburah and Chesed. The Secret Order consists of Binah, Chokmah and Kether. Each Order has a point of transition where consciousness is supposed to change not only in quantity but in quality.

In the scheme above Dr. Regardie does not have a Chakra for Malkuth, the Bride. If the student prefers, she can view Malkuth as part of the Muladhara Chakra.

The reader will note that in describing the chakras I start with Sahasrara and move to Muladhara. I have done this intentionally, as it attempts to demonstrate our belief that Ajna and Sahasrara are where we normally live, but in fact the unenlightened live only in Muladhara. We are born head first but the tail "wags the dog."

The purpose here is to get the reader to start from the top and work down, realize the fallacy and then to read again the entire section from the bottom up. Thus the second reading of the Chakras should start from the bottom of the section and work its way back through the book until the reader reaches Sahasrara again. This method will help the reader gain a deeper respect for the process she/he is about to undergo.

CHAKRA ASSOCIATIONS

(A chart summing up the associations to the various Chakras is provided in the appendix of this book.)

Sahasrara: Beyond all other Chakra Centers. Gross biophysical association/location: above the head. Technically not a Chakra, though many call it one. It might be considered Kether mixing with Ain or Ain Soph (Limitless Light). This center is beyond language. It implies the Sleeping God before

division: Brahman. Union as metaphor cannot be comprehended, however, during intense Tantra sessions it can be
dimly remembered after returning to ordinary consciousness.
It is beyond all opposites and moral codes — the origin of
notions of Chaos and Order.

Quoting Dr. Spiegelman again:

"When we come to the ultimate aim of the Kundalini Yoga
endeavor, the place of fulfillment, Jung is surprisingly
laconic. Here is what he says:

'To speak about the lotus of the thousand petals, the
Sahasrara center, is quite superfluous because that is
merely a philosophical concept with no substance
whatever for us; it is beyond any possible experience. In
Ajna there is still the experience of the self that is appar-
ently different from the object, the God. But in Sahasrara
it is not different. So the next conclusion would be that
there is no object, no God, there is nothing but Brahman.
There is no experience because it is one, it is without a
second. It is dormant, it is not, and therefore it is nirvana.
This is an entirely philosophical concept, a mere logical
conclusion from the premises above. It is without practical value for us.'

"Thus speaks the Jung of 1932, consistent with his long-held
theory that without an ego it is pointless and ridiculous to
speak of experience. Self without ego is a mere 'concept.' One
wonders how the Jung of twenty or thirty years later (he died
in 1961) would have described this. One returns again to his
dream of discovering himself as a yogin, meditating in a
temple, with his ego as an object of the yogin's dream. Would
this have changed his view? It is hard to say, but one would
guess that he would then emphasize the paradoxical nature
of the experience wherein the ego is both totally relativized
and 'nothing,' yet it is the 'all' which is flooded with
Brahman and, therefore, 'everything.' But here, in his psychological seminar, he is trying mightily to remain empirical, conceptual, comparative.

"Purnananda, on the other hand, devotes eight full verses
to this chakra which is beyond all chakras, and his commen-

tator, Kalicharana, engages in many paragraphs of distinction of names, concepts, this and that, just as if he were giving us a specific recipe which can be fulfilled only in the prescribed manner ...

"... at Sahasrara, not only are there no longer any animals or elements, as was the case in Ajna, but now there is not even a condition of principles (tattvas), nor strictly speaking, any Shiva or Shakti. At this point, Shiva is the Guru himself for our Saddhaka and the Shakti ... is Nirvana. Shunyata, the Void, is achieved, in which all being is no longer being. There is full union of the opposites ... and duality is overcome.

"The 'lotus of 1,000 petals' is a kind of mandala, but this vastly differentiated totality is both symbol and concreteness, is no longer located 'inside' the body but is on top of the head. All the letters are here, supreme bliss, void, supreme light, formlessness. The bliss here achieved is a consequence of Atman realized. Once fully here, furthermore, the yogin has no further need of rebirth and, if he does not die on the spot, he will not re-incarnate when he does die."

The Final Transition

Ajna: Gross biophysical association/location: between the eyebrows. Relates to the region of the "Mind-Ether." The color is white. Beyond the notion of dimensions ... The pure Mind ... Divine Union of personal self with the Collective Self ... Power to leave the body at will ... The ability of the True Seer. Kether on the Tree of Life is implied here.

"At this level, after a long development and differentiation in which the petals of the lotus increased, we now face a reduction. The petals are reduced to only two, and there is no mandala, no animal, and no element. For Jung, when there is no animal there is no bodily reality; only psychic reality exists. In short, the yogin now realizes himself as a psychic content of God.

"In the beginning, at Muladhara, God, or Atman was dormant and the yogin (ego) was aware. Now that God is fully awake, the ego realizes itself as a mere fragment, focused on the *union mystica*. This is symbolized in the presentation of the original Lingam, once more, but now white. In Vishuddha, furthermore says Jung, psychic reality was opposed to physical reality. Here in Ajna, there is no longer any physical reality, only psyche obtains.

"In his final lecture (IV) of his series on Kundalini Yoga, Jung takes up what he considers to be a paradox between the views of India and Hinduism and those of us in the West, particularly as this affects our understanding of Ajna. He does this by interpreting Sthula (which we have translated as the concrete or gross bodily level) as the personal aspect of consciousness, whereas the Suksma (which is generally translated as the subtle-body dimension) is the supra-personal. Jung suggests that each chakra has a sthula or personal aspect and a suksma or supra-personal aspect. Muladhara, for example, is in the pelvis but represents the world. We, in the West, think of our consciousness as in the head, at Ajna, but we live in Muladhara, in earthly entanglements and causalities. We are also identified with consciousness, and thus speak of 'sub-consciousness.' All this, however, is strictly from a sthula (personal) aspect. To look at things from a supra-personal aspect is suksma. We begin in the head, it is true, but we do not remain there. India and Kundalini, on the other hand, do entirely the reverse. Indians begin with the suksma aspect, even in Sahasrara, and conceive of man from the top down. We think of ourselves in Ajna, but we live in Muladhara. Here is the paradox:

"From the sthula aspect: India is in Muladhara, we are in Ajna.

"From the suksma aspect: India is in Ajna, we are in Muladhara.

"We shall return to this differentiation, but now, as we discuss Ajna, it is well for us to grasp this strange condition in which we 'think' with our heads but do not come to the impersonal aspect of ourselves, and the Indian does not so think, yet he is fully aware of the impersonal aspect of himself.

"All of this hinges on the fact that this chakra is the seat of the Tattva of Manas, or the mental faculties. This is stressed in the commentary and also it is noted that there is an additional, minor chakra, said to exist between Ajna and Sahasrara, also devoted to mental aspects. Our whole understanding of mind, in short, is what is at stake here.

"Avalon tells us that Ajna is called 'command' because at this point, the Saddhaka receives commands directly from the inner Guru, from above, in both the 'manas' minor chakras, and from the Sahasrara itself. All else recedes and loses significance. There are only two petals of the lotus now, and all the letters of the previous petals are exhausted. The mantra, now, is om, the ultimate, and fire, sun and moon converge. Here the Atman shines lustrous like a flame, and the yogi gains the final siddhis (powers) which permit him, at his death, to voluntarily put his prana at this spot and enter Purusha directly, needing no longer to re-incarnate.

"The Goddess here is '... like the moon (beautifully white).'

"... 'The excellent Yogi at the time of death joyfully places his vital breath (Prana) here and enters, (after death) that Supreme, Eternal, Birthless, Primeval Deva, the Purusha, who was before the three worlds and who is known by the Vedanta.'

"When all of this is accomplished, we learn ... that the yogi will then see, above the Ajna Chakra, the form of the Mahananda, and will make manifest pure Intelligence (Buddhi). From this point, there is no other task than to enter into the Sahasrara."

Vishuddha: Gross biophysical association/location: the throat region ... the invisible or false Sephiroth of Daath on the Tree of Life ... Relates to Sound and Ether ... The color is smoky purple. Power: freedom from possession by worldly activities; complete knowledge is obtained of the past, present and future. The mandala is a circle. The animal is the White elephant. The organ is the mouth.

"For Jung, the attainment of the Vishuddha Chakra is to reach the level of Psychic Reality. The element of this chakra, ether, is a substance which is not substance; it is a conception of substance. It is at a level of abstraction, therefore, which goes beyond the empirical world. The evolution of the

yogin's work, then, has him move up from the gross matter
and earth of Muladhara, all the way through the five
elements, now including the final one of ether. This ancient
idea of transformation is also found in alchemy, says Jung,
and hinges on a kind of cooking process. Manipura, with its
'handles' resembles a pot, which is like the cooking process
found in the 'kitchen' of the stomach, the region where that
chakra is located. If Manipura is the center of transformation,
via the emotions, then Anahata, which is the place of transformation and is invisible, provides the psychic foundation
which is fully realized, at last, in Vishuddha, the region of
psychological reality.

"Jung thinks that civilization as a whole has reached
Anahata — our center is no longer in the diaphragm as it was
with the Greeks. Despite this growth, however, we have not
yet reached Vishuddha, with its conception of the world as a
psychic reality. Only here can one grasp the Purusha, dimly
felt in Anahata, in which the essence of man is seen as a
subjective condition. Jung thinks that when the abstract ideas
of modern physics and of analytical psychology are generally comprehended, then civilization will have reached this
level of understanding."

[Note by Dr. Hyatt: I can only agree with Jung if we view his
statement in terms of a mountain with a broad base and a
narrow tip. From my point of view only the *notion* of Anahata
is contained in our present development; *the realization* of
Anahata is only reflected by a very few individuals. The fact
that only a few individuals have reached this point should not
necessarily reflect on civilization as a whole. From my
perspective, civilization still operates at Muladhara, while
believing it is operating at least at Ajna. For me, this disparity
does not imply aspiration except for a few, and is in fact the
'cause' of much pain and misery.]

"There is, then, a great gap between the achievements of
Anahata and Vishuddha. To reach the latter, thinks Jung, is to
unlearn all that was achieved in the progression from
Manipura to Anahata. At this point, the world itself and
everything in it becomes internal, psychical. To be at Vishuddha is to be with the subjective level of existence: everything

that happens to one's self is one's self. Or, to see it in another way, the world is a reflection of the psyche.

"This progression of the development in psychic reality, says Jung, can be seen by the changes in the animals which belong to each chakra. The elephant, like the horse, is, at Muladhara, both the instinctual urge which supports consciousness, and the cultivation of the will to enlarge it. The Makara, or Leviathan at Svadhisthana is the strongest animal in the water, just as the elephant is on the land. These two, in Jung's opinion, are really the same animal ...

"As we continue up the scale, we come to the ram of Manipura, the animal of fire and passion. Here sacrifice is central, we give up being mere slaves to our passions and desires. The result is to be found in the animal of Anahata, the gazelle or antelope. This animal is like the ram, but is not domesticated nor is it sacrificed. It is fleet and shy, light as air, and has lost the heaviness of earth. Only here, at last, is a psychic factor realized. It is like the unicorn (Holy Ghost) and bespeaks a psychic factor not even vouchsafed in Freud.

"When we come to Vishuddha, at last, we arrive at a level of instinct which transcends all the foregoing, for now we experience a purified condition of instinct (white elephant), in which the power supports human thoughts. Like Plato, there is an appreciation of the subjectivity of the mind, but not just as in intellect. The intellect requires physical evidence for its conceptions; not so the psyche itself, which does not. Consider, for example, the image of God! Finally, as we shall see later on, there is an absence (in Ajna), of the animal itself — there is only psychic reality. But here, at Vishuddha, we are in the realm of pure concepts, where the world is itself an inner drama.

"This is commensurate with the Hindu idea that word and speech are beyond tangible reality ...

"... the Goddess here, who is the Shakti Shakini. She is white, and carries a bow, arrow, noose and a goad. No longer frightening, she still conveys the power, like her consort, to urge the Seeker onward, to continue in his meditation and attain the Akashic level of consciousness. The Saddhaka's senses are now pure and controlled ...

"Avalon, in his scholarship, has provided here an additional verse (31A), not noted by either Purnananda nor Kalicharana, but by one Bala-deva in another text. In this verse, the yogi is 'in his wrath, able to move all the three worlds. Neither Brahma nor Vishnu, neither Hari-Hara nor Surya nor Ganapa is able to control his power (resist him).' Avalon makes no comment on this strange assertion of the power of the yogi, but we may here relate this to the attainment of psychic reality: when all existence is relativized in the psyche, then the Gods themselves no longer have power, and the meditator can grasp the essence behind the Gods themselves. This, in effect, is the last-but-one step for the yogi to come to the 'place of command' in the next chakra and discover that with all power comes no power, and that the yogi himself is nothing more than a psychic content of God."

Anahata: Gross biophysical association/location: the heart region ... Relates to the Air ... the sense of touch and feelings ... The color is blood red. The power of hearing with the inner ear of OM; power to protect and destroy the three worlds. The mandala is the familiar hexagram, or the Star of David. Note here that the Triangles are symbolic of the mixing of the Female and Male principles. It is the yearning for Union which reaches its sublime quality here. On the Tree of Life we see Tiphareth, the point of the Spiritual Heart, symbolized by the Inner Order of the Rosy Cross. The aspirant obtains the rank of Adeptus Minor, again a Neophyte, but this time in a new way. The animal is the antelope, a more gentle animal. The organ is the penis.

"For Jung, the Anahata chakra is where individuation, as a conscious awareness of the Self, truly begins. Until this point, one is immersed in desire, passion, the thousand-and-one things of existence there is, above all, no detachment. Here, at last, begins reason, a capacity to rise above the emotions. Here, too, one gets the first germ-like glimpses of Purusha, the thumbling of the Self. But one must remember, says Jung, that as long as we are mortal, we can become quite inflated by thinking that we have 'arrived' in Anahata; in point of fact, we remain in Muladhara with our egos, but we can and do behold Purusha in Anahata as we gaze on it from below.

For this, we truly need the mantras, the sacred words, because our capacity for true civilization, for the spiritualization of ourselves, is quite weak ...

"... The mandala now is a hexagon (combining the triangles of masculine and feminine nature), the petals of the lotus have increased to twelve, the animal is less demanding and aggressive, the element (air) is more 'spiritualized' and the Tattva or principle is significantly changed. In contrast to the previous cohesion, contractions, and expansion — all of which keep one contained in a single place — we now have the aspect of movement, which allows one to proceed outside of one's previous condition.

"Furthermore, we are told that the element here is Air, and the animal is the fleet-of-foot antelope ... who is truly gentle in comparison with the previous ones. As we shall see, even the Goddess is less violent here, for her 'heart is softened by the drinking of nectar.'

"Finally, we are informed that a small, secondary lotus is located just below this heart chakra. It is called a 'mental lotus,' with eight petals, in which there is the Kalpa Tree, a jeweled altar surmounted by an awning and decorated with flags. I have elsewhere [*The Tree of Life: Paths in Jungian Individuation*, Falcon Press, 1993] described this as a 'Buddhist Lotus,' since serenity is specified at the base of this Tree, and 'detachment,' is achieved."

"The Saddhaka who meditates on this Heart Lotus ... 'becomes like the Lord of Speech and like Ishvara, he is able to protect and destroy the worlds.' He is no longer subject to the whims ... of his own passions and now, by the grace of the Word, can himself both protect and eliminate ... Indeed we are told ... that the yogi so arrived 'is dearer than the dearest to women...'

"The God and Goddess here are indeed changed as well. Isha is the Shiva aspect here, with three eyes ... He wears gems around his neck and bells on his toes, as well, and possesses the 'soft radiance of ten million moons.' Even the Goddess, here called Kakini, becomes 'exhilarated and auspicious, benefactress of all.' Despite the fact that She still carries a noose and skull, she 'makes the sign of belling and the sign which dispels fear.' Her heart ... is softened ...

"Kalicharana informs us that this softening is caused by the supreme bliss engendered by drinking the nectar which drops from Sahasrara. In any case, her heart 'expands with the supreme bliss.' One might also add that this Kakini is thought of as wearing the skin of the black antelope. Does this not suggest also that She, too, has been civilized?

"With Jung, we can conclude that what was begun below in Muladhara is now achieved in Anahata. It is notable that this capacity to come to the impersonal aspect of one's Self is located at the 'heart' region, and even has, below it, a 'mental' lotus. To think with the heart, as the Pueblo Indians also know, is to truly have consciousness. This is no mere mental activity, as we shall later see."

A Very Important Transition Takes Place Here

At this point we move above the lower Chakras. As we enter Anahata, the Bride of The Son is redeemed and they begin the process of further transformation and the metaphorical absorption into Sahasrara (Kether), implying both Nuit, Brahman, and Ain Soph in the beyond.

Manipura: The Gross biophysical association/location: the diaphragm-navel region. Relates to Fire ... The Sense of sight and "emotions..." The color of heavy rain clouds, dark blue ... Power to create and destroy worlds and the wealth of personal knowledge ... The mandala is the triangle. The animal is the ram. The Organ is the anus. The lower portion of Tiphareth implied as one enters the Order of The Rosy Cross, on the Tree of Life. The path of the Portal Grade. Strong aspects of Philosophus as well, as he leaves Netzach consciousness.

"There is more development, differentiation and complexity, we might conclude, as well as more intense movement, symbolized by the fiery element on the one hand, and the mandala of triangles. Muladhara, with its order and clarity, gave us a mandala of the square; the Crescent-moon faced us in Svadhisthana and here we are confronted with the triangles of Manipura. The triangle, like the number three, is a dynamic figure, and the condition herein portrayed is equally dynamic. Within the triangles, furthermore, are to be found three swastikas. These symbols did not, in the day of Kundalini, convey the horror of our modern associations, yet it is not by chance alone that this chakra is connected with destruction, as we shall shortly see.

"First, however, we need a view of its various conditions. The animal here is the ram, a symbol of battle and power, as well as Rudra, the Shiva-form here, who is seated upon a bull. Clearly, power is indicated. Furthermore, the tattva condition is Expansion in contrast to the Cohesion of Muladhara and the Contraction of Svadhisthana. Expansion must mean the enhancement of energy and power, as well as consciousness. The qualities of heat, sight, and the 'organ' of the anus, confirms this paradox of conditions which add energy and vision (consciousness), yet produce detritus and destruction.

"The Bija of Fire is called 'Ram'. This is a seed mantra, seated on a ram, a carrier of Agni, the Lord of Fire. Here, too is Red Rudra, smeared with white ashes, and his Shakti Lakini who is 'fond of animal food.' This, Avalon informs us, is a digestive center, in which the Saddhaka is expected to satisfy the appetites of this devata, Lakini. We are still in the region of desire, and the seeker continues to eat meat, a practice given up at the later chakras.

"The verses of Purnananda tell us clearly that power and destruction are the conditions to be dealt with spiritually at this chakra ...

"This presentation of the 'destroyer of creation' is also ambivalent, just as fire is. We are faced with passions, which Jung tells us are indeed the fullness of jewels, but also Hell. If we cope with these passions, are able to get objectivity, then we rise above the ordinary situation of action and reaction, of belly-psychology, and can achieve calm perspective (the property of the next chakra); otherwise we roast in the Hell of our own fires.

"... Kalicharana informs us that this goddess Lakini is 'fierce of aspect and with her teeth protruding.' He continues:

'... in her right hand She holds the thunderbolt and the Shakti (the weapon of fire), and in the left She makes the gestures of dispelling fear and granting boons ... She is fond of meat and breast is ruddy with the blood and fat which drop from Her mouth.'

"Not a pretty picture, but a potent one, and here, too, the opposites come into play. All in all, this chakra is a clear representation of the Power principle, when viewed psychologically ... In any case, all of the 'lower' chakras confront us with instinctive conditions and passions, through which we must move in meditation and contemplation, in order to achieve the promised bliss and consciousness of 'higher' chakras. Yet we must remember that the flow of the Kundalini energy is, at last, a circular one and that the energy which rises also returns and there is circulation in the ultimate stages, even though this is not emphasized in many texts."

Svadhisthana: The Gross biophysical association/location: slightly above the genitals, below the naval. The Sense is taste... The color is vermilion ... Relates to Water. The power of well-reasoned discourse, or verse; imagination ... Freedom from enemies ... The mandala is the crescent. The animal is the alligator. The Organ is the hand. Relates to Yesod on the Tree of Life.

"Just as the Muladhara is the 'root support,' the beginning of a process of spiritual growth, rooting in the culture into which we are born, the next phase of development — after meditation and raising the energy — is to the 'proper place,' the region of the water. We have also 'risen' from the earthy condition of the perineum, between anus and genitals, to the 'root' of the genitals in the hypogastric region, the bladder. After earth comes water, after awakening from ordinary life comes 'baptism' or immersion in the spirit.

"It is Jung's genius here, to understand this second step of spiritual growth as an immersion in the sea of the unconscious. What for the East is 'up' for us is 'down.' Furthermore, what for the East is masculine (the moon), for us is feminine. He notes, prophetically as it turns out, that these symbols are made by men, and that it is masculine psychology with which we deal. All the same, he notes that in all initiation rites and mystery cults there is a kind of baptism, descent into water, and so it is here. The way of higher development leads through water, the immersion into our own depths.

"What is it that we find there in our depths? Why it is the makara fish, a kind of legendary animal, which we might compare to a crocodile, or better, the Leviathan of the Bible. That devouring monster confronts us, I think, with our desire, our lust, our never-ending demands that are never satisfied. It is these klesas or desires which are being transformed in the meditative work of the yogi, as he focuses on the Shiva-Shakti, god-goddess who dwells here.

"First of all, he finds the Shiva condition of Vishnu, in the form of youth. The spirit-form has grown from the child-like condition in Muladhara to the youthful one in Svadhisthana. The principle (tattva) under which he operates, however, is one of contraction. There is a narrowing of consciousness, from one point of view, and a submersion of that which had shown before as light. Now the hand is necessary; one not only stands on the common ground, one is actively engaged and molding one's own psyche as one struggles with the desire and lust which are activated herein. This same youth, who is also a symbol for the time when our own lusts are activated, is called upon as Hari (remember Hari-Krishna?) who is prayed to, as Purnananda tells us ...

"Kalicharana also tells us ... that this ... cleanses us from ... egoism, but also includes many of the evil inclinations such as Kama (lust), Krohda (anger) etc. We are dealing with the problems of lust, anger, desire and egoism.

"The Goddess, terrible to behold with her three-eyes and fierce projecting fangs, is what we fear and why we need the protection provided by her consort, the youthful Vishnu-Hari. Yet this Goddess, confronted and worshipped, ultimately frees us from the darkness and grants us boons. It is clear that, in our words, the confrontation of the unconscious with genuineness and respect brings about a transformation in the fierceness of our own desire-life and carries us onward on the path of spiritual development.

"Jung talks about the destructive aspect of the unconscious itself and it is here, in this struggle, that the truth of this is revealed. Also made manifest is the necessity of the first phase, the orderliness and regularity of a society in which the gods are worshipped and the rituals of existence hold sway. Yet without an encounter with this fierce Goddess, there is no fulfillment of the creativity suggested in the first chakra and the development of the mandala (from four to six petals) would not take place. It is noteworthy that there are six enemies of man, symbolized here by the meditation on the lotus. These are the greed and anger mentioned earlier, along with Moha (delusion), Mada (pride), Matsarya (envy), which all arise from a sense of 'mineness,' (Ahamkara). When overcome, the darkness of ignorance is replaced by the Sun of knowledge ...

"Is it only our own darkness which is overcome, or is it the darkness of the gods (nature) which is also being transformed?"

Muladhara: The Gross biophysical association/location: the genital/anal area. Relates to the earth ... The sense is smell ... The color is crimson ... The power of Speech and eternal knowledge. The mandala is the square. The animal is the elephant. The organ is the feet. Malkuth on The Tree of Life. She is the Bride of Kether and the furthest away. The Grade of Neophyte. The densest point of Matter, yet containing the seeds of Kether.

Dr. Spiegelman says of Muladhara,

"Jung's interpretation of the psychological meaning of this center is that the Self is asleep and the ego is conscious. He is thinking, of course, of the statement that the Kundalini Herself, wrapped three and one half times around a central lingam, a phallic energy source, is slumbering and that She is Herself a symbol of the Self, ever-present but needing to be awakened. Our ego, however, is conscious, insofar as we are living our everyday lives. We are 'rooted' in the earth, the element of this chakra, and safely seated on the elephant, Airavata. The elephant in India is a symbol of strength, firmness, solidity ... Not only are we rooted and supported by the earth, we are under the principle (tattva) of cohesion, of hanging together, and connected with that earth reality by our feet, and also by our sense of smell, like the animals.

"Our Mandala is four-square, and solid, our connection with life is through the institutions into which we are born. It is Jung's genius to interpret this as the condition of everyday consciousness, in which we are awake only in a collective sense; our true Selves are asleep."

"... the state of the Goddess, the Dakini who dwells here ... is deeply red, four-armed, holds a sacrificial spear, a sword, a skull-staff, and a drinking cup. She is powerful and bespeaks the need for suffering and sacrifice of everyday life, one thinks. She is far from asleep herself.

"Her consort, furthermore, in his Shiva aspects, is the Child-Brahma, who also has four hands, holds a staff, gourd, and rosary. He makes the gesture of dispelling fear. The spirit form (Shiva) here is a mere child, but he holds the community symbols of containment and prayer and aids us in dispelling the fear of the forces of the Gods and Kundalini, when aroused. So it is that the 'banality' of everyday life contains the powerful forces of the universe. The gods are not so fully asleep, but reveal themselves to us in their contained condition.

"The promise of the as-yet-unawakened Kundalini is shown very powerfully by ... Purnananda, who tells us of the sleeping of the Kundalini ...

'She is the world-bewilderer ... Like the spiral of the conch-shell, Her shining, snake-like form goes three-and-a-half times around Shiva and her lustre is as that of a strong flash of young strong lightning. Her sweet murmur is like the indistinct hum of swarms of love-mad bees. She produces melodious poetry and ... all other compositions in prose or verse ... It is She who maintains all the beings of the world by means of inspiration and expiration, and shines in the cavity of the root (Mula) Lotus like a chain of brilliant lights.'

'By meditating thus on her who shines within the Mula Chakra, with the lustre of ten million Suns, a man becomes Lord of speech and King among men, and an

Adept in all kinds of learning. He becomes ever free from all diseases, and his inmost Spirit becomes full of great gladness. Pure of the disposition by his deep and musical words, he serves the foremost of the Devas.'

"This is the promise of that as-yet-unawakened Kundalini, but it is significantly to be noted that the Creation is the specific suggestion here. Out of the ordinariness and the suffering of everyday life lies the possibility of the creation, of the rousing of energy and consciousness which makes one 'lord of speech' and 'adept of learning.'

"Jung ... suggests that the Kundalini is that which makes you go on the greatest adventures. It is, itself, a symbol for the divine urge. It is the 'lady' for the Knight, and the anima for the man. It can be a spark, a fear, a neurosis, anything which indicates that a greater will than our own intervenes in our life ...

"All of the foregoing sounds very unique and individual, yet Jung asserts that this is no personal task. No, it is impersonal; the energy itself is transpersonal and if we awaken it, we must be careful not to identify with it lest we suffer inflation. It happens to us as much as we cultivate it. Once more, the paradox becomes manifest: the divine is unconscious, we are unconscious of it; we awaken it, it awakens and the sorting out process begins."

Note: The locations of the Chakras given above reflect spheres of psycho/bio/spiritual energy, which in fact are more sublime than the physical regions mentioned. However, by focusing on these areas you will achieve proper results. Again, let the reader practice the method and be less concerned with EXACT meanings and associations.

CHAPTER EIGHT

THE JOY OF SEXUAL ECOLOGY

Melting into Love/Power is the purpose of the Great Work. If you have Christian notions that power is evil, or if you believe that Sex Magick is evil, then these techniques are not for you. Power is the force of the Universe. The Goddess *creates and destroys.* GOT IT?

Many "occultists and mystics" are preoccupied with verbal/hysterical distinctions between White and Black Magick. There is no such division except in Christianity or similar slave philosophies. No matter what a person calls his personal practices, be it prayer or magick, its purpose is to gain Power to serve self- and (SELF-) defined ends. This is not evil; it is Self-Realization and Planetary Psycho-Ecology. The planet is healed each time you do an intentional act. Every intentional act creates a specific type of consciousness which "feeds" the Universe. When an intentional act is coupled with a great force such as sex, enormous amounts of Conscious energies are created and the Universe rejoices.

Good and Evil are concepts which are created from the psycho-physical realities of pain and pleasure, power and powerlessness, and nothing more. This is based on our bio-structure.

Power is a neutral concept. What you use it for and how you interpret its use is up to you. If you even begin to use the words of Black and White, Good and Evil, you have lowered yourself and have entered the realm of Thud where Squeaky Things will afflict you with fear and trembling. Good and Evil are self-serving concepts which are required when the ego is under tension or attack. In the beginning and in the end there is simply Love/Power actualized through intentional efforts.

The purpose of the rules below are to increase the probability that you will be successful at the work. They contain no "moral" injunctions or sanctions.

The purpose of these movements is to intensify bio-spiritual energies; learning how to tolerate great energy and then how to move that energy according to your desire. Once you have accomplished this you then can call upon this power at will and direct it to your highest ends.

It is important to remember that during these practices you are stimulating various *body organs* and *brain centers*. You are, in fact, doing something real to yourself. So-called sexual/ emotive energy is the essence of all deep change and power. This energy may be used for dream work, insights, healing or whatever you choose. This is left completely up to you.

While practicing these methods do not moralize on your activities. Do not discuss your work with others as it will drain your energy and in the end simply confuse and inhibit the practice. Remember the motto of the New Aeon is *DO-IT*.

RULES

1. No genital intercourse is allowed during the practice of the preliminaries.

2. During these sessions only masturbation or oral stimulation is allowed.

3. You may begin sexual work as soon as you have learned the first set of exercises described in Chapter Six.

4. Genital intercourse is allowed once all of the preliminaries have been accomplished. This will take several months.

5. If the partner is a wife or husband, or steady partner be sure to separate the practice from your normal sexual activity by at least two days.

6. Choose a partner who will not romanticize the Tantric work, as this will hinder the deeper archetypal Love that develops.

7. These sexual movements should be practiced no more than twice a week.

THE BEGINNINGS OF THE EXCHANGE

The Mixing Of Forces

(Instructions for the *Lesser Banishing Ritual of the Pentagram* and the *Middle Pillar* — referred to below — are given in Chapter Nine and in the Appendices.)

Bathe. Dress in simple, soft, white garments.

Begin by performing the Banishing Ritual in the area in which you will be working.

Practice the Middle Pillar for 10 minutes with your partner. Hold hands or make sure that your bodies are touching.

Meditate on the Anahata (heart) chakra for 10 minutes. Do not control your thoughts or excitement.

You may light incense, burn candles or use lights or soft music to enhance the mood. Prepare the room in which you are working with the symbols, colors, sounds, etc. of the Chakra you are working with; i.e., for the Muladhara Chakra, a crimson curtain, a square Mandala, a statue of an elephant, etc.

Touch your partners hands and vibrate *OM* for 5 minutes.

Remove your gowns.

The female lies on the bed in the breathing position described before. She begins to breath as described, gently tilting her pelvis forward on the inhalation, toward her head. With every exhalation be sure the "AH" sound is made and the pelvis is dropped. After ten minutes of intense breathing, she stops the pelvic tilt and, while continuing deep breathing, her partner begins to stimulate her genital area with his hands, a vibrator, or his mouth. Timing and control are very important. *The major part of the stimulation must occur with the exhalation.* The rhythmic breathing must be kept up through the entire session.

When the female is about to reach orgasm her task is to focus her attention on the Chakra being worked — in this example, Muladhara. When orgasm is reached her focus must be on the Chakra.

The idea is to allow the energy of the genitals to move to Muladhara both physically and symbolically at the time of orgasm.

If she is capable of more than one orgasm per session or if it takes her less than 15 minutes to reach orgasm another practice session is desirable. However, the entire session should not last for more than 30 minutes.

Now the male assumes the breathing position and everything is done the same way, except that he should be kept from reaching orgasm for at least 25 minutes. This assumes that he can not have multiple orgasms of equal intensities. If he can have two orgasms of more or less equal power, this is permitted.

Once these practices have been performed for the first center for one month, you may begin to focus the energy on the next Chakra, the second region, then the third and so on. When all Chakras have been worked (one month for each), you may begin the next set of movements which include genital intercourse.

Each Chakra should be worked two or 3 times a month. If this is not possible, extend the program out far enough to accomplish this goal.

As you begin to work your way through each of the Chakras you will begin to experience very subtle changes in your life. Sometimes these are experienced as anxiety. Anxiety is a signal that there is *change* taking place of which you are unaware, or of which you have awareness but are holding on to. Do not concern yourself with this, just keep up your practices. From time to time you might want to return to the preliminary work, to help dissolve chronic anxiety and tension. In fact some individuals keep up the preliminary work throughout the entire Chakra workings. I wholeheartedly recommend this.

CHAPTER NINE

THE TAROT TRUMP CARDS AND TANTRIC INTERCOURSE

In this chapter I will describe how to create the proper settings for combining the Tarot symbols with your Tantric practice. There will be 22 Tantric intercourse sessions spread over six months to one year depending on time, availability and other personal considerations.

Special "empowered" days such as the solstice and equinox are ideal; however, other significant days such as birthdays are also excellent for this practice.

Incense, music, light and tasty food as well as small amounts of alcohol are important accompaniments. (Over the years I have found three or four ounces of wine, etc. to be useful in helping one to relax into this type of work.) The sounds, lights, and smells will vivify and *enhance* associations to the particular Trump card of the Major Arcana with which you are working. Case's book on the Tarot will provide the necessary intellectual clues to help you along.

Start with card #21, the World. Meditate on its meaning for at least one day prior to your session and extract from it those symbols which help you to add dimension and meaning to the card.

On the day of the session you and your partner should dress in your special clothing (loose fitting garments of soft, white cloth are preferable), and prepare the area using the symbols, fragrance, lighting, etc., that you have selected to create the environment.

Now, meditate on the Tarot symbol for at least ten minutes. (The Crowley-Harris Tarot deck is recommended because of its robust energy, but the Waite or the Golden Dawn deck will do.)

Perform the Banishing Ritual.

Invoke the highest god name you know. You may choose one listed in the Middle Pillar or use **IAO** (ee – aah – oh). Vibrate the syllables of the name.

Both partners should lie down on the bed in the breathing position, tilting the pelvis forward on the inhalation and letting it drop and saying "AH" on the exhalation. This should be done for 15 minutes.

The couple should then stimulate each other orally or by hand until they both feel ready for the genital embrace.

Each session requires that the female sit on top of the supine male. (This is normally the easiest position for Westerners who have not become experts in Yoga.)

The female mounts the male; no movement is allowed unless the male's penis begins to lose its erection. During this time each participant begins to breath deeply as before. This should continue for at least 10 minutes. The breathing should be synchronized. The male and female energy should operate as one complete unit. During this part of the encounter the couple should meditate on the Tarot symbol (e.g., *The World* in the first session) or another symbol which both have agreed upon to represent the Tarot symbol in question. For example, a couple might agree on the image of the Buddha when working with the Lovers card. Some find using a God Image to represent the meaning of the card to be more effective. Remember each Major Arcana Card symbolizes a living energy form.

Now, movement may begin and each partner attempts to control orgasm for at least five minutes.

As orgasm is about to be reached your attention should be switched to the Chakra being worked with and at that time all sexual energy should be released. (See below for Chakra correspondences to the Major Arcana.)

The essence of the movement is as follows: The female should first raise herself on the exhalation, at this time the male should also slightly raise himself on the exhalation. On the inhalation the female should lower herself as the male lowers himself. There should be complete union at this time. After a few moments of this, with the female leading, she should begin to reverse this process. That is, she should lower herself on the exhalation, and raise herself on the inhalation. The male should follow suit. The couple should continue this until they can no longer control their breathing and movements. As they reach orgasm they should turn their attention to the Chakra in operation.

(Do not become discouraged if you are somewhat spastic and uncoordinated in attempting these exercises.)

After this phase is complete, the couple should rest quietly for thirty minutes, meditating on their highest aspirations and the meaning of the Tarot Symbol.

Each session is governed by a different Tarot symbol and Chakra. Start with the World and move backwards through the cards one by one ending with the Mage. Start with the Muladhara Chakra and move Chakra by Chakra ending with Sahasrara. When a Chakra cycle is completed, start over again with Muladhara Chakra.

The Fool card is not used until you have completed all the other cards and then only as described below.

SOME BRIEF ASSOCIATIONS TO THE TAROT MAJOR TRUMPS

Working the Paths of The Tree of Life

THE IMPERSONAL TRANSMUTATION OF THE FORCE(S)

There are 22 Major Tarot Symbols, starting with the Fool which has the reference of zero and is the Ultimate Beginning Force — highly undifferentiated. Counting the Fool as one symbol, 21 Tarot Symbols remain which are divided into groups of seven each. The first seven starting with the Mage are called the "Operating Principles." The second group beginning with the Strength Card are called the "Operating Agencies." The final group, beginning with the Devil are

called the "Manifested Forces." You will begin this work with
this last group.

If you arrange the Major Symbols in the following order you
will get an idea of how things work:

0
The Chaotic Whirling Force

1 2 3 4 5 6 7
THE PRINCIPLES

8 9 10 11 12 13 14
THE AGENCIES

15 16 17 18 19 20 21
THE MANIFESTATIONS

The example which follows is only an illustration. It is not
necessary to understand this in order to benefit from the
methods.

The Primal Force represented by the Fool is channeled
through each Principle which finds its way through an Agency
(a forming process) and finally Manifests itself as something
more concrete. Thus, the first Principle is the Mage, moving
through the Agency of Strength, Manifesting as the Devil
symbol. (Note that there are seven Tarot symbols for the
Principles, the Agencies and the Manifestations. Therefore
each Chakra is worked three times, one for each of these
categories.)

O Fool — Etheric Air — THE WILD CHAOTIC WIND
The Governing Force of the All
THE CHAKRA OF NO-NAME
The Hebrew Letter is Aleph
and Aleph's Number is One

Aleph is the Hebrew Letter given to the Fool symbol and
Aleph's number is One. It is the undifferentiated spirit of
existence. The "Airy" almost aimless quality of life. The

Primal Force before it is directed. Think of yourself as a newborn infant and then begin to imagine the Explosion caused by the Sperm and Egg uniting. Also imagine the mad frenzy of the many Sperm, each yearning to penetrate the Egg.

Mage — Mercury — Chakra #7

The Hebrew letter is Beth. (Value is 2). The planner and director of the World, but not its creator. Think of yourself as a crawling, exploring infant.

High Priestess — Moon — Chakra #6

The Hebrew letter is Gimel. (Value is 3). The death of the personal ego. The archetypal force of the Divine Goddess. A vessel in the highest sense of the word. The Mother of the Self. Think of yourself sucking at Mommy's breast.

Empress — Venus — Chakra #5

The Hebrew letter is Dalath. (Value is 4). The sexual quality of the Goddess. Here in the form of attractiveness, a bit more personal in this sense. Aphrodite. Reproduction in all its meaning and levels. Think of your love for your mother and her love for you.

Emperor — Aries — Chakra #4

The Hebrew letter is Heh. (Value is 5). War, strife, conquest, force, ambition, power. Think of your father and your feelings for him, etc.

Hierophant — Taurus — Chakra #3

The Hebrew letter is Vau. (Value is 6). Teaching, rational process, learning by explanation. Think of the first time you felt guilty or ashamed.

Lovers — Gemini — Chakra #2

The Hebrew letter is Zayin. (Value is 7). Forces arising from the power of inspiration and impulse. Learning by instinct and intuition. Think of the words you mispronounced as a child.

Chariot — Cancer — Chakra #1

The Hebrew letter is Cheth. (Value is 8). Triumph and victory through the regulation of opposite forces. The director.

Learning by doing, feeling and sensing. Think of the first time you made a machine work.

Strength — Leo — Chakra #7

The Hebrew letter is Teth. (Value is 9). Power unarrested. Competition, courage, with the ability to let go and move onward. Think of the first time you hid your feelings from others.

Hermit — Virgo — Chakra #6

The Hebrew letter is Yod. (Value is 10). Active inspiration. Divine wisdom from above. Think of your first masturbation fantasy.

Wheel — Jupiter — Chakra #5

The Hebrew letter is Kaph. (Value is 20). The wheel of fate. Conveys idea of karma, roulette, success. The feeling of being on top of the world. Think of your first hot love affair.

Justice — Libra — Chakra #4

The Hebrew letter is Lamed. (Value is 30). The goad, the whip, arrested power. Balanced forces, but lacking inspiration and joy. Think of your first boss, or of taking orders from above.

Hanged Man — Water — Chakra #3

The Hebrew letter is Mem. (Value is 40). The sacrifice of the ego, id and superego identification into the Abyss. Sometimes thought of as Christ sacrificing His personal Ego, to the Self. This act cannot be accomplished vicariously as is claimed in Christianity. No one can do it for you. Anyone who claims they can is lying, attempting to take away your right to know the Goddess personally by your own efforts. Vicarious salvation is disrespectful and demeaning to both Man and His Gods. Think of why you became interested in Enlightenment.

Death — Scorpio — Chakra #2

The Hebrew letter is Nun. (Value is 50). Involuntary change as opposed to the Moon symbol. Transformation. Think of your body out of control of your mind.

Temperance — Sagittarius — Chakra #1

The Hebrew letter is Samekh. (Value is 60). Combining forces, working through the process of realization. Think of what Tantra really means.

Devil — Capricorn — Chakra #7

The Hebrew letter is Ayin. (Value is 70). The powers of the material forces. Note the two human figures are free to slip off their chains, yet they are fixated on what they believe and see. Simply a symbol of restriction on any plane of consciousness. An invention of limitation. Obsessions based on fears. Learning through restriction, fear and anxiety. Think of ESP and precognition.

Tower — Mars — Chakra #6

The Hebrew letter is Peh. (Value is 80). Ambition, fighting, courage. The transformation of the self forced by living in an extreme. Learning by opposites. Think of how synchronicity might work.

Star — Aquarius — Chakra #5

The Hebrew letter is Tzaddi. (Value is 90). Hope. The future. The multiplicity of union. Many small pieces of light make up the illusion of light itself. Learning step by step without losing the image of the whole. The future. Think of Higher Intelligence speaking to you.

Moon — Pisces — Chakra #4

The Hebrew letter is Qoph. (Value is 100). Voluntary change. The secret qualities of the changing forces of mood and will opposing and combining. The phases of personality. Think of what Jung means by the Shadow.

Sun — Sun — Chakra #3

The Hebrew letter is Resh. (Value is 200). Glory. The moment of realization. A passing point on the road to silence and wisdom. Think of Osiris Risen, Christ, Rebirth.

Judgment — Fire — Chakra #2

The Hebrew letter is Shin. (Value is 300). An awakening from the sleep of assumed wakefulness. The realization that we can wake up with the help of our own dual nature. Giving up of stupidity and death as our only options. Think of a new model of eternity.

The World — Saturn (Earth) — Chakra #1

The Hebrew letter is Tav. (Value is 400). Completion, the world of unity, at the level of the Kingdom. Think of Out-of-Body-Experience.

BE SURE TO BEGIN YOUR WORK WITH THE WORLD

Adept students who have completed the work as described will begin to work out other magickal relations among the Chakras, the Tarot symbols, the Middle Pillar and the Tree of Life. These methods can be used to deliberately create changes in the psyche, as well as in the world. For example what might be the relationship of working with Ajna and the Star symbol as compared to the Devil symbol? How could each be used to affect your life, and what insights might be developed?

THE GREAT THUNDER: THE ULTIMATE ORGASM

When you have completed working all of the Tarot Symbols (Paths of the Tree) through the Mage, then and only then may you work the energy of the Fool and the CHAKRA of No Name.

To begin, breathe deeply, and then roll yourselves up into two balls. Imagine that you are both formulating the energy necessary for the creation of new worlds. Hold this position for at least 3 minutes, then expand yourselves manifesting the energy you have both created. You may let out a yell if appropriate.

Perform the Lesser Banishing Ritual of the Pentagram
(Refer to the Appendix for additional instructions)

The Kabbalistic Cross

Facing east:

Touch your forehead and say **Atoh** (aah - toh).
Touch your Heart and say **Malkuth** (mal - kooth).
Touch your Right Shoulder and say **Ve-Geburah** (veh - ghee - boo - rah).
Touch your Left Shoulder and say **Ve-Gedulah** (veh - ghee - doo - lah).
Touch your Heart and say **Le-Olam** (lee - oh - lum).
Point the symbolic dagger inward and say **Amen** (aah - mayn).

Still facing east:

Trace the Banishing pentagram and vibrate **Y H V H** (yoad - hay - vaahv - hay), as you thrust your symbolic dagger into the heart of the pentagram.

With your arm still extended, turn to the South:

Trace the Banishing pentagram and vibrate the name **ADONAI** (aah - doh - noy). [Remember to thrust the symbolic dagger as you vibrate each God name].

With your arm still extended, turn to the West:

Trace the Banishing pentagram and vibrate the name **EHIEH** (eh - hayh - yay).

With your arm still extended, turn to the North:

Trace the Banishing pentagram and vibrate the name **AGLA** (ah - guh - lah).

With your arm still extended return to the East, completing the circle.

Now imagine yourself surrounded in a Flaming Circle of four Pentagrams.

Stand straight with your arms out forming the shape of a Cross:

Before me **Raphael** (rah - fay - ale).
Behind me **Gabriel** (gah - bree - ale).
At my right shoulder, **Michael** (mee - khigh - ale).
At my left shoulder, **Auriel** (oh - ree - ale).

Then say:

Before me flames the Pentagram Behind me shines the six-rayed Star.

Finish by repeating the Kabbalistic Cross:

Touch your forehead and say **Atoh.**
Touch your Heart and say **Malkuth.**
Touch your Right Shoulder and say **Ve-Geburah.**
Touch your Left Shoulder and say **Ve-Gedulah.**
Touch your Heart and say **Le-Olam.**
Point the symbolic dagger inward and say **Amen.**

Now *invoke* using the same ritual described above. The difference is that you trace the pentagram differently. (See the Appendix.)

The Middle Pillar

In Dr. Regardie's copy of Wilhelm's *Secret of the Golden Flower*, 3rd impression, 1935, there are a number of passages underlined. As Dr. Regardie was not a habitual underliner, we may assume that when he did underline, it was for a very good reason. One of the passages which he underlined more than once contained references to the circulation of light.

In the next method, the proper circulation of light is essential for the true magickal effects to occur.

Therefore it is urged that the partners should practice the ritual many times *prior* to including the sexual aspects. As a rule it is wise to practice this together holding hands or touching in some fashion.

The Great Whirlings

The male should be on his back and the female should sit on top of him. Move only when instructed, unless the penis begins to lose its stiffness.

Begin by imagining a *scintillating white light* about the size of a small basketball forming above the head and piercing the top of the skull. This is called the Kether point. Now vibrate the Divine Name **EHIEH** (eh - hayh - yay) as the sphere of Light grows brighter and more energetic. Do this for 5 minutes.

On the last six vibrations of **EHIEH** the female should move on each sound of the word.

As the force of this whirling ball of power becomes exceedingly real for you and your partner, allow the energy to descend slowly through the head. Allow it to rest in the throat or Da'ath point. Here imagine a *lavender color*. Vibrate the Divine Name **Y H V H ELOHIM** (yeh - ho – vah ale - oh - heem) until the energy becomes exceedingly real for you and your partner.

Again on the last six vibrations the female should move 6 times.

Bring the energy down through the chest until it rests at the Heart or Tiphareth. Vibrate the Divine Name **Y H V H ELOAH VA DAATH** (yeh - ho - vah el - oh - ah vah da - ahth). The color of light should be *golden yellow* growing brighter and clearer as you vibrate the Name.

On the 6 last vibrations the female should move 6 times.

Move the power through the diaphragm and abdominal region to the pelvis (Yesod), and vibrate the Divine Name **SHADDAI EL CHAI** (sha - dye el hi) visualizing a sphere of *deep purple.*

Here on the last 10 vibrations the male should move 10 times very slowly.

Finally, allow the energy to descend through the leg until it formulates at Malkuth, the feet. The Divine Name is

ADONAI HA-ARETZ (ah - doe - noy ha - ah - retz) and the sphere is *black.*

The male should again move 10 times quickly on the final vibrations of the holy name.

Now, draw the energy up from the Black light of Malkuth changing colors as described above as it ascends to Kether. When the light reaches Kether concentrate on the White brilliance of this region.

When the light is at Kether and your movements are complete, meditate silently for a few moments and then begin the circulation of white light.

Note: At times Dr. Regardie ignored the different colors of the Spheres and simply used the white scintillating light of Kether for each of the points. However, he and I agreed that the colored system is better suited for the practice of Western Tantra.

The Orgastic Circulation Of Light

Circulate the energy of the White Light as follows:

Allow it to *descend downward and outward via the left side* of the body *during every exhalation.* When it reaches the left foot, transfer the energy over to the right foot and allow it to *ascend the right side of the body on the inhalation.* This should be done at least 10 times. The partners should move slowly in unison 10 times.

The *second circulation* of energy begins in Kether and travels down the *front of the body on the exhalation* and then up the *back of the body on the inhalation.* This should be done at least ten times as well. The partners should move slowly in unison 10 times.

The *third circulation,* beginning with Kether, follows *down through the body on the exhalation* until it reaches Malkuth. The energy is *drawn up through the body to Kether on the inhalation.* When it reaches the Crown, imagine it to discharge like water from a fountain at the end of each inhalation. The fire and sparks of this scintillating fountain go up and out through the Crown and then descend down and encompasses the body on the exhalation. After the final circulation has been completed and the fountaining maintained for a few movements, the couple should begin moving and breathing heavily as they surround themselves with sparkling light. The movements should then become spontaneous and at the moment of orgasm the light should be gathered and thrust beyond Sahasrara, toward the Chakra with No Name.

The Crystallization Of The Light

The orgastic Light of the Chakra of No Name may be likened to the Philosopher's Stone, The Golden Flower, or the Lotus. It is a body of light created by the process of transmutation of spiritual-sexual energy. This is an experiential realization, thus, the proof of the pudding is in the Doing and Creating.

The process of transmutation requires the proper balance and mixing of heat/cold, passive/active and white/black. In a broader sense we are using tremendous active forces to create a non-active force. The nurturing we provide the womb-child through our practices creates a worthy resting place of deep silence for the aspirants involved in the-creation process.

The circulating of orgastic light is no doubt one of the most beautiful secrets of the Great Work. As the light circulates again and again and your practices become more powerful and refined, a crystallization occurs and you begin to form the magickal child. Whether you choose it to be physical or spiritual or both, the creation of this spirit body allows you to have contact with the forces of the higher Spiritual Body. You have not only opened the doors of perception, but can now begin the process of real action in a way unknown to those who lack this initiation.

CHAPTER TEN

THE MAGICKAL CHILD

Dr. Israel Regardie believed that these techniques could be used by advanced students to incarnate "spiritual" energies on the physical plane, as well as making important shifts in the orientation of the Psyche and the Universe. In other words, if these methods were used properly, couples could bring into the world "divine" forces in the children they generated, who could influence the future of the race.

In this sense Dr. Regardie was advocating a new form of birth control. Like myself, he believed that we have had enough dross, and it is time to go for the gold. However, we were both aware of the fact that unless enough individuals took it upon themselves to do the work consciously we would have to continue "feeding" the Universe in our primitive mechanical ways. These included such things as wars, plagues and suffering in general.

In addition to creating "real children" these methods could be used to create "psycho-spiritual vessels," which would shift the focus of the mind as well as develop new powers and abilities.

We knew that these principles and practices would never be taken up by the ordinary person and thus we had little need to worry about blunders in that area. Only those individuals with great determination and persistence would even attempt to enter the Hall of True Initiation. While Dr. Regardie believed in indulgence in the highest sense, he knew that the act of transcendence could only occur when the Root instincts were freed from the compulsions of civilization and finally transcended.

This did not mean that physical enjoyment would cease. It simply meant that another component would be added to the Root instinct once the compulsions created by society were removed. This is why he recommended that aspiring "seekers" undergo therapy and other forms of treatment, of which this book and its practices are an example.

To use these techniques for the purposes of occult eugenics it is essential that you have followed all the instructions outlined previously.

The creation of the magickal child by ritualized sexual practices is symbolic in one sense of the whirling forces of nature, mixing and separating in their chaotic dance of creation.

Man's working with the basic forces of nature allows conscious co-operation and co-creation with the cosmos, and she/he becomes a miniature form of the cosmic process following its root laws.

By willful and conscious cooperation man increases and refines his energies, sacrificing himself willingly to Nature instead of being a passive food source in the food chain. The realization that man's emotional, physical and sexual energies are food for the "Gods" can create great personal turmoil at first, however, when one begins to joyously participate in this spiritual feeding frenzy, one is "elevated perpendicularly to infinity," as Crowley wrote.

SELECTING THE SYMBOLS
YOU WISH TO MANIFEST

"Know then that as Man is born into this world amidst the darkness of Nature and the strife of contending forces, so must his first endeavor be to seek the Light through their reconciliation. Thus, thou who hast trial and trouble of this life, rejoice because of them, for in them is strength, and by their means is a pathway opened unto that Light Divine.

"How should it be otherwise, O man, whose life is but a day in Eternity, a drop in the Ocean of Time? How, if thy

*trials were not many, couldst thou purge thy soul from the
dross of Earth?"*

To "purge thy soul from the dross of Earth" means to stop
feeding the Universe mechanically.

Easier said than done? Well, yes and no. We begin to purge
the earth of its dross by the act of transcendence and by
actualizing our True Will, through discipline and intentional
"suffering." This last phrase is often misunderstood. I understand intentional "suffering" as conscious work aimed at
developing a "real I." Often this requires going against the
automatic processes of mind/body which many individuals
find painful. It is the opposite of struggle and indulgence.

USING THE TAROT SYMBOLS ON A DAILY BASIS

Your personal Tarot symbols are determined by analyzing
your birth date. They are the karmic forces or energies you
were born with, and must contend with from birth throughout
most of your life. It is important to work with these symbols
first as they will set the stage for what is to come.

The Tarot symbols of your birth are pictorial and thus have
a greater impact on your conscious and unconscious mind
than mere concepts and words. They serve the purpose of
stimulating the transcendental process.

When I speak of the transcendental process I am more
concerned with the *process* than with the content of what is
transcended. This attitude is more objective than that of
dogmatic morality and ultimately more useful. For example,
it matters not whether eating or sex or opening a door with
your right hand is transcended; what matters, is that
consciousness becomes fully aware that transcendence is
possible.

My position has sometimes been regarded as amoral or
immoral by conventional western religions. On the lower
planes of man's functioning as an insect, this is no doubt
correct: I am undermining hive morality and hive discipline.
On the higher planes, however, this position is highly moral.

The Tarot symbols of the minor arcana are ideal for teaching the transcendence process in a practical fashion.

YOUR PERSONAL TAROT SYMBOLS

Make your personal Tarot symbols a part of your consciousness, and note their operation in your daily activities.

Begin looking at the symbols which precede and follow your birth symbol in the Minor Arcana, as these make up your *"karmic-genetic file."*

Later on, focus on the symbols which precede and follow you in the Major Arcana. Though these are highly abstract and archetypal, they will give you clues into the nature and plans of your Psyche. I will describe this in greater detail later.

When attempting to understand and become more familiar with the Court Cards, it is wise to reflect on the natural opposite of your birth card. Thus, if you are a Queen of Cups, note the nature and action of the King of Cups.

DETERMINING YOUR SYMBOLS

The Court Card Symbol/The Personage

— If you are a female, and 40 years or older, you are a Queen force.

— If you are under 40 and female, you are a Page or Princess force.

There is nothing sacred about the age 40. You may be a Queen force at 20, or a Page/Princess force at 60. Use the above rule and then decide which fits you best.

The same holds true for men. An older male is a King and a younger one is a Knight. (In Crowley's deck, the older male is the Knight, and the younger male is the Prince.) Use the 40 rule and then decide for yourself.

Court Forces And Elements

If you are a Water sign and a female under 40 you would be a Page of Cups in the court cards. Over 40 makes you a Queen of Cups. If you are a male and a water sign you would be a King of Cups if over 40 and a Knight of Cups if under 40.

If you are an Earth sign are a male over 40, you are a King of Pentacles. Under 40 makes you a Knight of Pentacles. If you are a female and an earth sign over 40, you are a Queen of Pentacles; under 40 makes you a Page of Pentacles. If you are an Air sign and a female over 40, you are a Queen of Swords; under 40 is a Page of Swords. If you are an Air sign and male over 40, you are a King of Swords; under 40 makes you a Knight of Swords. If you are a Fire sign and a male over 40, you are a King of Wands; under 40 is a Knight of Wands. If you are a fire sign and a female over 40, you are a Queen of Wands; under 40 is a Page of Wands.

Find the court card which symbolizes you and write it down in your Tarot journal.

Note: According to Dr. Israel Regardie (1984), Knights sit on Thrones, and Kings ride on Horses. (This maybe one reason why Crowley changed King to Knight and Knight to Prince.) Some decks have these reversed so as to confound the user. Make corrections on your symbols if you so desire.

The Elemental Forces: Signs and Decans

Note: D1 is the first decan, D2 is the second, D3 is the third. The number following D1 etc. is the date the decan begins. The ending date is the day before the next decan begins. The decans help you understand the specific qualities and nature of your spiritual energy. All of these dates are very close approximations. Verify them in a ephemeris, as there will be minor changes from time to time.

Wands are fire signs:

Aries, (D1 3-21) boldness, fierceness, resolution and shamelessness, (D2 4-1) pride nobility, wealth and rulership, (D3 4-11) subtlety and beauty.

Leo, (D1 7-23) boldness, liberality, victory, cruelty, lust and violence, (D2 8-3) love, pleasure, society, carefulness, (D3 8-14) ignorance, pretended knowledge, wrangling, victory over the low and base, the drawing of swords.

Sagittarius, (D1 11-23) boldness, freedom, welfare, liberality, fields and gardens, (D2 12-3) fear, worry, lamentation, grief and anxiety, (D3 12-13) ill-will, levity, envy; obstinacy and swiftness in all evil activities.

Cups are water signs:

Cancer, (D1 6-22) science, love, mirth, subtlety and magistry, (D2 7-3) pleasure, mirth, abundance and plenty, (D3 7-13) acquiring goods, pursuing, contention among people.

Scorpio, (D1 10-24) strife, sadness, treachery, deceit, ill will, (D2 11-4) affronts, detection, stirring up of quarrels, science, (D3 11-13) war, drunkenness, fornication, wealth, pride and rage against women.

Pisces, (D1 2-19) thoughts, anxiety, moving from place to place, seeking of riches and food, (D2 3-1) high mindedness and great ideals, (D3 3-11) sex, peacemaking and pleasure.

Swords are air signs:

Gemini, (D1 5-22) writing, calculations, giving and receiving money and wisdom in unprofitable things, (D2 6-2) burdens, pressure, labor, subtlety, dishonesty, (D3 6-12) disdain, mirth, and many unprofitable words.

Libra, (D1 9-24) justice, aid, truth and helping the poor, (D2 10-4) gluttony, following lowly pleasures, (D3 10-14) quietness, dance, ease, plenty, the good life.

Aquarius, (D1 1-21) poverty, anxiety, grieving after gain, never resting from labor, (D2 1-31) beauty, dominance, conceit, good manners and self-esteem, (D3 2-10) abundance and compliments, detection and affronts.

Pentacles are earth signs:

Taurus, (D1 4-21) building, planting and earthly wisdom, (D2 5-1) power, nobility, rule over people, (D3 5-12) misery, slavery, necessity, madness, and baseness.

Virgo, (D1 8-24) planting, colonizing, collecting and storing money and food, (D2 9-4) gain, covetousness, hoarding, (D3 9-14) slothfulness, old attitudes, and loss through compulsions.

Capricorn, (D1 12-22) wandering travail, labor and joy, gains and loss, weakness and necessity, (D2 1-2) seeking the unknowable, (D3 1-12) covetousness, suspicion, careful ordering of matters but with discontent.

Minor Arcana Signs

Your personal symbol in the Minor Arcana is determined by your complete birth date. For example December 15, 1947, would be 12-15-1947.

Enter your birth date in your Tarot Journal. Now begin reducing this date to a number from 2 through 10.

Aces, the number 1, do not count as they are primal and represent undifferentiated formulating energies.

Each Ace symbol evolves through an entire process of development, as reflected by its transformation from one number to the next in the sequence 2 through 10.

Each number from 2 through 10 is a stage of manifest energy which has its own meaning and developmental attribute.

For an in-depth understanding of this phenomena, study the glyph of the Tree of Life (See *The Complete Golden Dawn System of Magic*, 1984, Falcon Press.)

Begin with your own suit, by placing each Root Card or Ace, one at a time on position number one, the Crown. Then follow with symbol number 2 of that suit, etc. Study and reflect on the developmental process, from the undifferentiated to the final manifestation. Start with the Ace of Wands (Fire), move to Cups (Water) then to Swords (Air), and finally Pentacles (Earth).

These are associated with the Four Worlds of the Kabbalists: Atziluth (Fire-Wands-King-Force), Briah (Water-Cups-Queen-Force), Yetzirah (Air-Swords-Knight-Force), and Assiah (Earth-Pentacles-Page-Force). As you study these you will discover how your own personal minor arcana symbol relates to the Tree of Life and to the Universe at large. This will help you to discover and understand your True Will.

Energy Names On The Tree And Tarot Card Numbers

The first three energy centers are archetypal:

Kether are Aces — The Crown.
Chokmah are 2s — The Father.
Binah are 3s — The Mother.

Gedulah are 4s, think of Jupiter.
Geburah are 5s, think of Mars.
Tiphareth are 6s, think of the Sun.
Netzach are 7s, think of Venus.
Hod are 8s, think of Mercury.
Yesod are 9s, think of Moon.
Malkuth are 10s, think of Earth.

Note: the Tree of Life consists of three pillars with three energy centers on the outer pillars (the left pillar contains Binah, Geburah, and Hod; the right pillar contains Chokmah, Gedulah and Netzach; and the middle pillar includes Kether, Tiphareth, Yesod, and Malkuth). The middle pillar has certain energy centers similar to the Chakras: Kether is often thought of as the Crown, Tiphareth the Heart, Yesod the Generative functions, and Malkuth the Physical body, or Earth.

Reducing The Birth Date To Find Your Personal Symbol

For example if your birthday is 7-12-1943, your number is 9: (7 + 12 + 19 + 43 = 81; 8 + 1 = **9**).

If your birthday was 9-11-1966, your number is 6.

You find your number by adding: 9 + 11 + 19 + 66. This equals 96. Then continue adding until a number from 2 through 10 is reached: 9 + 6 = 15 and, finally, 1 + 5 = **6**. *Check your addition at least 3 times.*

Let us reduce the date 1-15-1988. 1 + 15 + 19 + 88 = 123. 1 + 2 + 3 = **6**. The number is 6. Try five more dates until you get the procedure down.

Remember that the astrological signs are related to the symbol energies in the following fashion:

Cups are water signs: Cancer, Scorpio, Pisces

Wands are fire signs: Aries, Leo, Sagittarius

Swords are air signs: Gemini, Aquarius, Libra

Pentacles are earth signs: Taurus, Capricorn, Virgo

Using this information and the numerical reduction method described above, we arrive at our personal Minor Arcana symbol as follows:

My birthday is 7-12-1943. I am a Cancer, therefore I am a Cup. Reducing my birthday to a number from 2-10 gives us a 9. (7 + 12 + 19 + 43 = 81; 8 + 1 = **9**). I am a **9 of Cups.**

Now let us try Dr. Regardie's birthday. He is a Scorpio and thus a Cup. Reducing his birthday, 11-17-1907, gives us a 9 also. (11 + 17 + 19 + 7 = 54; 5 + 4 = 9). Dr. Regardie is also a **9 of Cups.** Although we are both 9 of Cups, there is also a great deal of difference between us based on our Signs, Major Arcana Card, and Decans.

Let us try this birth date, 12-25-0000. Summing these we have 10. (12 + 25 = 37; 3 + 7 = 10). As this birthday is Capricorn, an Earth sign, we have the **10 of Pentacles.**

Now try this with your birth date and write it down in your journal. Next, calculate your parents' birth dates and two other individuals who are close to you.

Finding Your Archetypal Symbol in the Major Arcana

Here again, your birth date is the key element. Note the astrological signs and their relationships to the Major Symbols:

For the Sign:

Aries: The Emperor

Taurus: The Hierophant

Gemini: The Lovers

Cancer: The Chariot

Leo: Strength

Virgo: The Hermit

Libra: Justice

Scorpio: Death

Sagittarius: Temperance

Capricorn: The Devil

Aquarius: The Star

Pisces: The Moon

If, for a moment, you can imagine a force starting somewhere in the Universe and finding its way down to a single point, you will get a sense of the Archetypal energy moving its way from the Major Symbol, to the Court Symbol, to the Root symbol of the Ace and then down to your personal symbol.

To apply this to a specific case, I will use my birth date which is 7-12-1943. I was born under the sign of Cancer, and thus I am the Archetype of the Charioteer. I am also the King of Cups, because I am a male over 40, the ace of Cups because I am a water sign and the 9 of Cups, because I am a water sign and my birth date reduces to 9.

In my Journal I would write down the following after my birth date:

Major Symbol: The Charioteer
Court Symbol: The King of Cups
The Root Symbol: Ace of Cups
Personal Symbol: The Nine of Cups
Preceding Personal Symbol: The Eight of Cups
Progressive Personal Symbol: The Ten of Cups

The preceding Minor Arcana symbol gives you a sense of where you are coming from, and the progressive symbol tells you where you are going. For example, my preceding symbol is the 8 of Cups and my progressive symbol is the 10 of Cups. As the nine, I am in the middle, moving about these three symbols. This can tell me much about how I function and the events of my daily life.

Once you know your three symbols in the minor arcana, you can begin to create a story about your situation.

For example, as the Charioteer I am archetypically involved with Triumph and Victory over certain powerful forces. The issues of Victory and Triumph are very important to me and in this phase of my life (over 40) I attempt to manifest these through Venusian qualities. I am deeply involved with Tantric

Love, writing, the arts and science. I am very enthusiastic, capable of great extremes of emotion. I have to guard against obsessions with sex, idleness and exaggerations.

The 9 of Cups indicates again that I am impulse-guided. I desire complete material success, and I am capable of gluttony and extreme self-indulgence. I am concerned with collecting power and having my every wish satisfied.

The 8 of Cups indicates that I sometimes abandon much of my material pre-occupation for a new beginning. Frequently this indicates a spiritual quest or taking up the occupation of healer.

The 10 of Cups indicates that I am blessed by good fortune, and perpetual success. However, this pertains to the future. It will only manifest itself when I am capable of controlling and modulating my more undifferentiated energies.

Determining your three cards if you are a 10 or a 2 is a little different. If, for example, you are a 10 of Wands, your past card is the 9 of Wands, but your next card is the 2 of *Cups*. This is based on the rule of descending worlds. (Do not get inflated or deflated by the words "ascending" or "descending.") The four worlds of manifestation are:

Fire
Water
Air
Earth

Thus moving down from the suit of Fire (Wands) you move into the suit of Water (Cups). In the case of the 10 of Wands, the balancing symbols of the past and future would be the 9 of Wands and 2 of Cups respectively.

In my opinion, this is the finest way to study the psycho-spiritual notion of karma. In fact, students who use these symbols in a proper fashion and who also generate a large amount of free will can move through all of their lives in one lifetime and free themselves from the wheel of birth and death.

In practice then, if we assume that we all start from the world of Fire (Wands) and move to the world of Earth

(Pentacles), pentacle people may be closer to finishing their tour of duty than any of the other suits.

However, some believe that the Fire people (Wands) are closer to finishing their tour than any other.

Since this is a model which no one can scientifically verify, the safest method is to learn to live the life of each symbol in the minor cards.

Before we can do that, we must, however, become completely familiar with our own birth card, and our immediate past and future.

CHAPTER ELEVEN

CREATING
THE MAGICKAL CHILD

Once you are familiar with the Tarot and have determined the Minor Arcana, Court cards and Major Arcana symbols for you and your mate, study and meditate on these for a week.

Next you will select the qualities and energies you wish to incarnate in a living spirit or magickal child. Because you will use the Minor Arcana to represent these energies, you need to be thoroughly familiar with the Tarot.

For example, say you wish the child to have the qualities of the 2 of Cups. You know that the water signs are Scorpio, Cancer, and Pisces. Write down the qualities of each of the water signs and their respective decans and meditate on them. Then choose the preferred decan for each of the signs and rank them as first, second and third choices. Say you wish the child to be primarily influenced by the first decan of Cancer. *Look up the qualities and write them down.* You will then be ready to construct a Ritual as explained below.

BRIEF MEANINGS OF
THE MINORS & COURT CARDS

Since my training has been in the psychological and sociological aspects of the human condition, I tend to view each of the Minor Arcana symbols as representative of the types of experiences and orientations a person can have in life. Some of the given meanings cannot reflect the impact that these images have on the mind. In my opinion these images are the best representation of the character, learning experiences and the ups and down of life. Equally important are the "solutions" they provide for the human condition.

Wands: The Intuitive Person

Ace of Wands:
Root of fire, force, strength, sudden acceleration.
The realm of spirit, creation and energy.

2 of wands: dominion, power over one's sphere and territory.

3 of wands: established strength, fixed and entrenched, an aspect of arrogance.

4 of wands: perfected and exemplary work, that which endures, equilibrium, balance and harmony.

5 of wands: strife, clashes and discord with a farcical or absurd quality; impotent, feeble and inept conflict. Compare with the 5 of Swords.

6 of wands: victory after stasis; triumph and fulfillment, gain and success.

7 of wands: valor and fortitude in the face of opposition; however, this may be a false battle, or one created by one's own unconscious temperament. (This card was the designated symbol on 12-7-1941=79=7W, Pearl Harbor Day.)

8 of wands: swiftness, arrival of information with haste, capricious and flighty quality; falling to earth.

9 of wands: magnificent strength, outstanding force, health, energy.

10 of wands: great oppression, burdens, malice, revenge. Here one must learn to calm the mind when oppressed, and take one thing at a time. Magnificent strength has now turned into a burden. What was missing for this to happen?

King of wands: active, generous, fierce, sudden and impetuous; if ill-dignified this becomes evil-minded, cruel, brutal. [Note: "Ill-dignified" means that the cards next to the card at issue exert a negative influence.]

Queen of wands: steady force applied, attractive power; kind and generous when not opposed; if ill-dignified, the force is domineering, revengeful, and tyrannical. This Queen can be a betrayer!

Knight of wands: usually he is noble, quick, hasty, strong, violent, but just. If ill-dignified, he is cruel, intolerant, prejudiced and ill-natured.

Page of wands: brilliance, courage, beauty, force sudden in anger or love; a desire for power; enthusiastic; and revengeful. If ill-dignified, superficial, theatrical, cruel, unstable and domineering.

Cups: The Feeling Person

Ace of Cups:
Root of water, fertility, productiveness, beauty,
pleasure and happiness. Creative energy of the
heart and emotions.

2 of cups: love, friendship, marriage; positive emotion, with a quality of courage.

3 of cups: abundance, merriment, joyous friendship; a very feminine energy.

4 of cups: pleasure, luxury, gifts given and received; but some tension always present. Indicates a change in life orientation. Indecision; doubt; Hamlet's hesitation.

5 of cups: loss of pleasure, disappointment in relationships, nostalgia for the lost things of the past. A person crying behind closed door.

6 of cups: empty pleasure, childhood dreams fulfilled. A tendency to live in the past. The joys and games of childhood. The drifter or Flower child.

7 of cups: illusory success, weakness in a position of power, lies, deceit, flattery. There is a strong aspect of self-deception. Believing that the ego is capable of handling responsibility when it is not.

8 of cups: success abandoned ... new beginnings, sometimes moving toward the spiritual path. Often referred to as leaving material success for something higher, but not necessarily of ones own free will.

9 of cups: material success complete, wishes fulfilled, sometimes with over-indulgence. Pleasant and generous, but sometimes very moody and greedy (insecure).

10 of cups: perpetual success, good fortune, This can become very boring if a new challenge and a higher goal is not on the horizon.

King of cups: graceful, poetic, Venusian, indolent, but enthusiastic if aroused. If ill-dignified, he is sensual, idle and untruthful.

Queen of cups: imaginative, poetic, kind, but unwilling to take on the burdens of others, dreamy in nature, good in essence, easily affected by other forces, stronger in imagination than in feeling.

Knight of cups: is subtle, violent and crafty with an artistic flare. A fierce nature with a calm exterior. If ill-dignified he can become intensely evil. (Machiavellian) The Borgia Pope.

Page of cups: sweet, kind, poetic, gentle, imaginative, dreamy, at times indolent, yet courageous if roused. If ill-dignified, she is selfish and luxurious.

Swords: The Reasoning Person

Ace of Swords:
Root of air, an invoked force, a great power for good or evil,
strength through trouble, the affirmation of justice. The creative
energy of reason.

2 of swords: peace restored with minor tension.

3 of swords: sorrow, deep tears, emotional pain.

4 of swords: rest after strife, change for the better, a need for quiet time.

5 of swords: conflict: victory or defeat, slander, an active card, unlike the 5 of wands.

6 of swords: earned success, a journey ended, hard work leads to help and success. Indicates a need for movement or association with water, to balance the limitations of reason.

7 of swords: unstable effort, untrustworthiness: impulsive, greedy action. A symbol of deviousness if ill-dignified.

8 of swords: restricted force, petty difficulties; mental manacles; being imprisoned by one's own reasoning process.

9 of swords: despair and cruelty, illness of heart: Mind at the end of its tether: injustice unexplained. "Why do the nations rage so furiously together, and the people imagine a vain thing?" This card is worse than the following one.

10 of swords: ruin, failure, the final end of a matter, with the implied hope of a new beginning. The worst is over with. Reason has discovered its own end, its own limitations. Man is free from worshipping his logical faculty.

King of swords: active, subtle, clever, delicate, courageous; inclined to dominate; if ill-dignified, deceitful, tyrannical and crafty.

Queen of swords: highly perceptive, keen mind, very accurate in superficial analysis, quick, subtle; if ill-dignified, she is cruel, sly and deceitful, unreliable, although she puts on a good show.

Knight of swords: an idea man, he is distrustful, suspicious, firm in a friendship, careful, slow and over cautious. He can slay as fast as he creates. If ill-dignified, he is harsh, malicious, plotting, obstinate, and unreliable.

Page of swords: strength, and subtleness in material things. Grace in motion. She can be very frivolous and cunning when needy.

Pentacles: The Sensory-Sensual Person

Ace of Pentacles:
Root of earth, material in all senses, both good and evil. It shows material gain, labor, power and wealth. The creative energy of body and earth.

2 of pentacles: harmony in the midst of change, pleasant visits, holidays.

3 of pentacles: material work well done, commerce; sometimes a meeting with a teacher.

4 of pentacles: powers over the earth, receiving money but normally with an earthly purpose.

5 of pentacles: material trouble, loss of property or valuables for those outside of the great work which are assumed to reside within.

6 of pentacles: material success in business.

7 of pentacles: successful but unfulfilled, work without reward is successful; unselfish efforts lead to surprise results.

8 of pentacles: prudence, moderation, good skills in handling small matters.

9 of pentacles: material gain, inheritance.

10 of pentacles: wealth on the mundane level; however eventual boredom is very likely.

King of pentacles: unless well-dignified, he is lazy, heavy, dull and excessive, however he is laborious, clever and patient in material matters. When ill-dignified, he is an avaricious, grasping, dull, jealous and cowardly force.

Queen of pentacles: impetuous, kind, timid, of a good heart, intelligent but moody; if ill-dignified she is undecided, capricious, foolish, and changeable.

Knight of pentacles: solid, reliable and practical in applying his force, he increases the value of other forces; if ill-dignified he is stupid, animal-like and material. He is slow to anger, but when aroused is furious.

Page of pentacles: generous, kind, diligent, benevolent, careful, courageous, preserving, but sometimes pitiful. If ill-dignified, she is wasteful.

CONTINUATION OF THE SELECTION PROCEDURE

The 2 of Cups Example

You know that the Knight or Page of Cups will be the governing court cards depending on the sex of the child you wish to manifest. Remove them from the deck. You also know that the Chariot, Death and the Moon, in the Major Arcana govern Cancer, Scorpio and Pisces, respectively. Remove the symbol which you desire to manifest.

Now, say the year you choose to have a "magickal child" is 1990. The year 1990 adds up to the number 10. This is the number for all of 1990. Say the sign is Cancer, which is the number 6 for the June part of Cancer or 7 for the July part. For example, 6 added to 10 equals 16, which reduces to 7. If we used 7 for the July part of Cancer to 10 it would equal 17 which would reduce to 8. We now ask what dates in Cancer would give us the correct number which would add up and finally reduce to 2 to get the desired results of the 2 of Cups. For the number 7, which as you remember is obtained by adding the month June or 6 to the year 1990 (6 + 19 + 90 = 115 = 7) the date would be the 22nd of June. 7 + 22 = 29 = 11 = 2 of Cups, and the first decan of Cancer. The next date would be for the number 8. This is obtained by adding 7 (for July) to the year (1990) which yields a sum of 17 = 8. This would be July the 3rd: (8 + 3 = 11 = 2), and July 12th: (12 + 8 = 20 = 2), and finally the 21st of July, which would be 21 + 8 = 29 = 11 = 2. Be sure to note the decans if this is important for you. There are simple formulas for determining the correct dates. The aspirant should work these out on her own.

There are 4 dates in Cancer, June 22nd, July 3rd, July 12th, and July 21st which creates a force or a link which has the powers of the 2 of Cups. There will also be dates in Scorpio, and Pisces which will yield a 2 of Cups, but with different qualities.

The ideal days for conception to occur are now known. Remember conception and not the day of birth is the time when the ultimate influence of forces are determined.

This is more interesting when you consider that conception is often more pleasurable than the process of birth, and that during conception the forces of male and female energy are co-operative and highly charged.

Thus, in the process of "incarnating energy systems" into physical manifestation, the times of the most dynamic energy determine to a large extent what comes into existence. The time prior to conception, conception, and the time following, exert the greatest force upon the psycho-bio-spiritual forces materializing in human form.

By the practice of Tantric intercourse, meditation and timing, a highly charged energy field is set up, whereby proper concentration on the attributes of the desired entity (the Magickal Child) brings about the necessary force to increase the probability of its manifestation.

As you continue to study the methods, you can easily see how much concentration and energy you have put into the process. Not only do these methods help manifest the Magickal Child, they also change you and your partner's psycho/bio/spiritual nature.

The amount of energy expended into the creation of the Magickal Child also supports the notion of past, present and future elite "races". How many people do you know — or for that matter how many exist on the planet — who would spend the time creating a Magickal Child by conscious and deliberate means? The number probably would not populate a small town of 5,000.

Major Arcana Symbol & The Chakras

Now it is important to select the Major Arcana card which reflects the astrological sign under which conception will take place. We find that for Cancer it is the Chariot. The chakra for the Chariot is:

Muladhara Chakra — #1 Location: the anal area. Relates to the earth ... The sense is smell ... Color is crimson ... Power of Speech and eternal knowledge. Mandala is the square. The animal is the elephant. The organ is the feet. Malkuth on The Tree of Life. She is the Bride of Kether and the furthest away.

The Grade of Neophyte. The densest point of Matter, yet containing the seeds of Kether.

Prepare the room three days in advance. The Tarot symbols of the couple and the "magickal child" to be — including the court cards — should be placed prominently on an altar.

The area in which conception takes place should contain the symbols of the Chakra associated with the Tarot Symbol.

Once the area is prepared the couple should ready themselves by meditating on the highest divine name, performing the banishing ritual and the middle pillar ritual. *Follow a healthy diet — consisting of protein, natural carbohydrates, vegetables and fruit — for a least one month prior to beginning the work. Discontinue using all nonprescription drugs and eliminate the use of alcohol. Add a balanced supplement of vitamins and minerals and quiet your mind with meditation.*

Tantric intercourse using the Middle Pillar should take place one day prior to the correct day, on the correct day and one day after. The couple should have intercourse during this period as many times as possible; however it is essential that the act of intercourse be performed as described earlier. The energy must be shifted to the chakra in question in order to obtain the desired results.

The selection of the appropriate date in order to obtain the influence of the 2 of cups should be determined by the days the female is most fertile. I recommend that in this instance all the correct days be used, *starting* with the most fertile time, (usually thought of as beginning, for most women, seven days after menstruation ceases). Remember the primary importance here is the method and power of the Tantric act, which is determined by the Major Card and the Chakra, the court card, and finally the Minor Arcana symbol.

After conception has taken place, and the physician has determined the approximate date of delivery, the couple should continue the other exercises in this book, focusing their activity on the heart, throat and middle eye chakras. In other words, the energy should be cast in those directions throughout gestation. At least three times prior to delivery, once in each trimester the energy should be directed toward the region of Sahasrara and the Chakra of No Name, using the Middle Pillar Method. This will reinforce the entire process on the astral plane.

LIFE, DEATH & THE MAGICKAL CHILD

There is great Meaning in producing the Magickal Child, and it is a practical method for dividing, mixing and integrating the forces of life. In one sense a couple practicing this method are preparing for their own death/rebirth (transformation) experience. Through the division, mixing and integration of energy, they are creating psycho-spiritual forms which they can project themselves into at will.

The true mystic can begin to see the possibilities of "astral travel" and "eternal life," and the power of controlling reincarnation. In this sense the automatic processes of the wheel of life and death are placed in the hands of this new Ego, born from meditation, work and dedication. This new Ego, the Magickal Child, has powers which transcend our normal understanding of cause and effect, good and evil and desire and will.

She and He have "stepped out" of being an ordinary couple and have stepped into a world of magick and vision that is beyond what we know in our ordinary state of consciousness. No longer are they deluded by the fact that, in reality, they have lived in Muladhara while believing they have lived in Anahata, Ajna or Sahasrara. Thus, they are no longer unwilling participants in Karma. They know now that they are Ajna, and in fact are commanded by their own creation, the Magickal Child, or the *Guru of the Body of Light*. Yet this creation is not simply of the ego, but of something stronger — more primitive from the ego's point of view. Its source is once again realized as *Undifferentiated Desire*, moving through a process of differentiated desire back again to *Undifferentiated Desire*.

> *"That most excellent of men who has controlled his mind and known this place is never again born in the Wandering (Samsara, the world of birth and rebirth to which men are*

*impelled by their Karma), as there is nothing in the three
worlds which binds him. His mind being controlled and
his aim achieved, he possesses complete power to do all
which he wishes, and to prevent that which is contrary to
his will. He ever more moves towards the Brahman. His
speech, whether in prose or verse, is ever pure and sweet."*

This most tantalizing and interesting image focuses on power
and will, thus still emphasizing a form of uniqueness. Yet the
process of crystallization of the form of the Magickal Child
residing outside of the body indicates to us the notion of
Sahasrara and beyond. Although the above verse stresses that
re-incarnation is no longer necessary, the absolute statement
of having the power to do one's will indicates that the Adept
may now choose re-incarnation if she/he pleases. The reader
will note that this discussion of will and power is beyond any
notion of morality as ordinary humans attempt to live it on
the plane of Malkuth.

DEATH WATCH

One of the most important abilities to have when death is
about to approach is the ability to focus the mind on a point
and then empty oneself into it. As the adept can begin to see,
the creation of a spiritual magickal child is the ideal vessel for
this process. It simply parallels one purpose of having
children — personal immortality. The difference here is that
the spiritual Magickal Child does contain the reflective
consciousness of your Self.

As the couple becomes expert at creating magickal
children, they become increasingly aware of multi-faceted
possibilities of which a peculiar form of immortality is but
one.

It seems very strange to me that normal sexual intercourse,
the method for creating new members of the species would
not be seen as one method of creating spiritual children which
could be used as a vessel for containing the essence of their
parents.

No doubt many eastern practices were intended for this use, but due to translation errors or deliberate disguises, the idea of the magickal child has remained relatively hidden.

To crystallize from the shower of orgastic meditation an Entity which can serve as both a vehicle and source of guidance and information is in my view the goal of all true magickal and mystical orders.

In one sense this creation is a bridge between matter in its heaviest manifestation and matter in its finest form.

What makes the creation of the Magickal Child unique is the psycho-alchemical work required. The personal and inter-personal effort, coupled with the power of the sexual instinct, mixed with the meditative forces, creating a relativization of the ego — a process quite distinct from the popular notion that the ego must be destroyed. True understanding of the reality of the Psyche has taken place by and through the ego in its reflective sense. In fact this understanding has been there all the time, but experienced only in glimpses, for the most part remaining unconscious, and unreflected. Now the aware-ness is mirrored, reflected, but the ego does not take credit for the impersonal nature of the entire process. The sense of the personal is finally realized as a necessary illusion. The reality is that *the ego itself is an archetype.* "I AM" means the same thing, whatever "I" happens to say it. *The ego is not just a necessary illusion, but a **necessary illusion.***

THE SPHERE OF UNION

To gather a better glimpse of the results of these Tantric practices, imagine a spherical ball floating one foot over your head. When this is fixed in your mind, now imagine that you are inside that ball. Now visualize the ball as being wrapped by two thick bands of gold strips, one going from front to back and the other going from left to right. Now begin to create the fountain effect inside the ball as described in the Middle Pillar Ritual. Increase and decrease the fountain effect at will.

Begin to control the ball, by moving it around the room. Send it on a trip around the neighborhood, taking note of anything you see or experience. As you become more expert in traveling begin to send the Ball of Union on missions. Send it to a friend's house while she is sleeping. Enter into the person's dreams if you wish and plant helpful suggestions and ideas. If a person is ill, increase the fountain effect and transfer the power into the other person's Psyche. The possibilities are endless.

CHAPTER TWELVE

THE CARE & UPBRINGING OF MAGICKAL CHILDREN

Nothing concerning the process of conception should be discussed with the child until she/he is old enough to understand.

The child should be kept away from public school and all conventional religions which teach guilt, blind obedience and self-contempt.

Each society imitates the teaching style of its Brand Name Gods. Therefore, if you wish your child to be happy, healthy, intelligent and humane, keep her away from hateful God Images. Most of us in the West have had first hand experience with the negative attitudes which the Gods have had toward man. Most all of these have been passed on by the "adults" who cared for us. Remember, they were terrified by the same awful images. Also, in the West emotional abuse of children is so common that it still goes unnoticed. I would venture to say that emotional abuse is the number one "killer" of human beings, and the models of our Gods reflect this.

The environment should be enriched with lots of colors and educational toys including computers. The child should not be frightened or bullied by force or religious threats but taught self discipline when the timing is right. The parents should avoid hateful arguments, although creative arguments are acceptable for the child to observe.

Sports should be encouraged for its own sake. All efforts should be made to develop high levels of mental activities, social behavior, foreign languages, special skills. Most of these are best taught by allowing the child to imitate you or another who is more expert than the child. You should not force the child and if this seems necessary it is because you have not been a good example. Learning occurs best by observation and imitation.

Allow the child to take chances. Do not be over-protective, or project too much of your personal anxieties. Keep worries and complaining to a minimum. Avoid all forms of condemnation and other-worldliness. A child's mind cannot understand minute differences. It tends to think wholistically, thus any concept will be engulfed and not digested.

The child will learn ethical philosophy by observing how you treat others around you. Remember the model of the Tree of Life. Severity is sometimes necessary, Mercy is sometimes necessary and Mildness is sometimes necessary. Use your head. Think things out before over- reacting to situations.

Do not moralize with the child. Speak of actions and behaviors in terms of real consequences. Do not impart metaphysical concepts until the child is able to understand them and their uses.

Discuss social behavior, not from the point of view of "Thou shalt" and Thou shalt not", but as necessary things to learn and use. Again do not moralize or intimidate. Use role modeling and discipline. You are the best example, not your mother's or father's fictions, truisms, or axioms. Remember what a child becomes to a large extent is a function of what she learns at "the breast."

Allow the child to watch TV on a restricted basis. Instead of normal television, show movies which reflect excellence, heroism, achievement. Allow the child to make his own movies.

The best way to teach eating habits is again by allowing the child to observe your proper eating habits.

When the child comes home with questions concerning other people's lifestyles, inform the child that every person has the "right" to live as they see fit, but that some lifestyles are a bit better for assuring a happy and healthy life.

Observe what the child is automatically attracted to. Provide more of the same, but do not become discouraged if the child loses interest.

Breast feed the child for at least one year, but no more than 18 months. Do not start toilet training too early. Let the child observe you using the toilet. She/he will try to imitate you. Have the child completely toilet trained by two years old.

Play with the child as often as you can. Allow it to play with other children, but be careful about the adults you have supervise the child. Do not allow hateful humans to pour nonsense into the child's mind before it has developed the critical faculties to discern and differentiate.

While nudity is not a problem up to a certain age, in this culture it is wise to discontinue excessive displays of nudity just prior to age 5. Do not allow the child to observe intercourse. This is not a moral dictate, but a practical one. The child does not have the ability to understand what is really happening and she/he will jump to misunderstandings. Only give information when asked. Stop giving information when you feel the child cannot understand what you are talking about. Again, give factual and informed statements. Talk in a kind and friendly voice, and do not moralize. Generalizations are dangerous for the future of young children. Learn to be specific, following the rule, of Who, What, Where, Why, How and When. Children can relate well to these components of communication.

Discipline is essential, but it must be in the child's terms and not yours. Do not expect adult performance from children, because their natural behavior will often be better and worse.

CHAPTER THIRTEEN

LOVE

THE BIRTH OF THE NEW HUMAN

One day the Buddha was walking with Ananda, his favorite disciple. He was deeply engrossed in answering a question. A fly landed on Buddha's forehead and he vigorously shooed it away. At that moment he stopped what he was doing and repeated the act. Ananda asked him, "Why are you shooing the fly away again, when it has gone?" Buddha replied, "I was so engrossed in your question that I was unconscious of what I had done. I am doing it again, to know it consciously."

This is the essence of Western Tantra: "to know *it* consciously."

TO LUST AFTER BODIES

It is said by occultists that there are seven bodies: the physical, the etheric, the astral, the mental, the spiritual, the cosmic and the nirvanic. Some believe that these bodies are directly correlated to the Chakras.

Conscious immersion in the orgastic reflex changes each body into the next. These minute changes are frequently felt in dreams and meditation. With sufficient practice each of these bodies become crystallized and then finally disappear.

The transition from the physical to the nirvanic body will be reflected in everything you do, whether it is eating, communicating or working. Your entire orientation toward life will be transformed. Your reference points will begin to change. You will no longer see the Divine through the framework of your mind, heart or body — you will simply see it. You will begin to let things drop. You will stop referencing yourself to the past and the future. You will disappear into Love.

THE NEW PERSON

There is little Love in this world. However, there is much talk of it. Those who talk so much are in love with the idea of love; however, on closer examination they know nothing of it. If there were all this Love in the world then why is the world so unhappy? Why is there so much misery, frustration and madness?

The experience of life is born from frustration. This is inevitable.

The experience of life is born from conflict, and this too is inevitable. Somehow, somewhere, we have forgotten the rest of the formula. In the process of Life knowing itself pain is accumulated. We can ignore this pain by defocusing or we can use this pain as an opportunity to focus. If we choose to focus we can either focus on the pain itself, or focus on what the pain points to. Pain's finger *is* pointing *at* Consciousness and Love. They are the same.

Love can not be known as unconscious emotion or as a moral dictate. Each emotion lives in its own opposite and each moral dictate dies from its own compulsiveness.

For Love to be real it must be whole, radiant and living. It must possess a quality of being independent of objects. This can be brought about by the marriage of the male and female *in* the spirit of Godliness. This is a marriage of consciousness and unconsciousness in the presence of Self. This divine union of the King and Queen is experienced in the orgastic "wedding night" resulting in a New Child — the Magickal Child.

The Magickal Child is the New Human born not out of simple biological or cultural dictates, but out of Love itself. However, to experience this Love we must learn to let go of ourselves. This is not a moral dictate as told to us by our religions but a necessity for our survival as well as the planet. *Letting go of ourselves is the greatest Selfish act.* To be this Selfish is to find one's No-thing-ness. The Orgastic reflex can teach us this and the Magickal Child is the outward symbol that we are willing to suffer life, but *now* in a totally different way. Now we suffer but we *are not* the suffering. Now we see the ego, but we *are not* the ego. Love must be No-Thing. You must sit in it, be absorbed by it until there is no difference between you and it.

The Tantric act is *a giving and a receiving.* There is no taking. When giving and receiving reach their highest level of intensity then No-One is left. There is simply Love.

It is easier to discuss Love in the negative sense since being immersed in Love is beyond the subject/object duality and beyond time and space. Time and space are the ultimate sign-posts for logic, languages, definitions and philosophical systems. However, they are useless when we try to define Love.

Love is not rational, nor is it the yearning for some person. Love is the core element of the Universe. Those individuals who frequently talk of love know little of it. More often they are feeling the compelling need to give or to receive the impossible. More often they are speaking of control, guilt, loneliness or sex. Love is more; it is the compelling need to Merge — to Melt — to return to the Source. As the source is One, so must the Tantric couple finally disappear. What is left is simply Love itself.

The formula is simple. First there is Wholeness, then there is Division, then there is Wholeness. The second Wholeness is different from the first in that the major portion of it has to be earned. The remainder is added as a gift.

Ordinary life doesn't give us this opportunity and neither do our religions. We are too steeped in our needs and our ego. We are fighting off feelings of vulnerability, ineffectualness, loneliness and death. To return to the Source is an experience out of the space-time continuum. *It is without Thing-ness.* Unlike other experiences, however, when it reaches sufficient depth a crystallization occurs which changes our whole orientation toward life. We realize at once that we are nearing Home.

Although we are born with this sense, we lose it in the natural process of becoming adults. To become an adult we must learn division. We are taught that the other is not us, that she/he is a potential enemy. We are taught to hold on to ourselves, never to rest or to let go. We are taught to identify with the things for which we strive. We are taught to believe that language is reality.

Our relationships are frequently empty and hollow. More often then not, they reflect our need for status, for power and escape. We demand the impossible from ourselves and everyone else. We are asleep, sound asleep, being lived by our instincts and learned habits of behavior, yet all the time believing that we are awake, conscious and in charge.

Much of the misery in the world is the result of the frustrated desire to return, to melt, to merge, to be one. What I have presented in this book is one way of making the journey. It will only help you if you work at it. This does not mean that you have to give up living your ordinary life. It does require a few hours of work each week. At some point real change will begin to happen. You will crystallize into the being you have always been but have forgotten. You will merge back into the whole, this time not as an ignorant infant, but as an innocent person. Once this transformation has taken place you will no longer have to ask any questions. You *will be* the answer.

APPENDIX ONE

DIAGRAMS AND TABLES

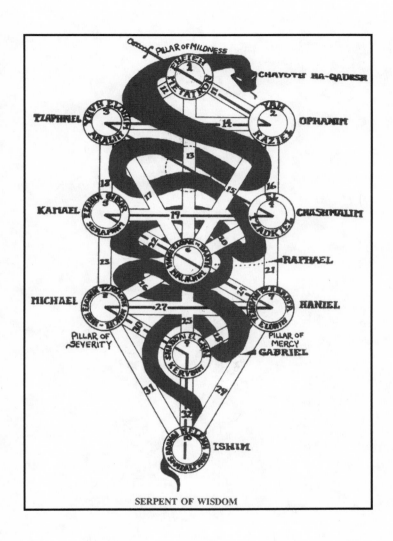

SERPENT OF WISDOM

BANISHING & INVOKING PENTAGRAMS

BANISHING

INVOKING

CHAKRA	SITUATION (Plexus)	PETALS	MANDALA	ANIMAL	TATTVA (sense-act)	SHIVA	SHAKTI	ELEMENT
Muladhara 'root support'	Perineum: between anus & genitals	4	Square	Elephant	Cohesion; smell; feet	Brahma child	Dakini	Earth
PSYCHOLOGICAL SIGNIFICANCE: Everyday reality; grown into; family, work, etc. Elephant, domesticated libido.								
Svadhisthana 'proper place'	Hypogastric; bladder, above genital	6	Crescent	Makara crocodile	Contraction; taste; hand	Hari-Vishnu youth	Rakini	Water
PSYCHOLOGICAL SIGNIFICANCE: Unconscious, devouring, dangerous, negative fish-monster. Moon.								
Manipura 'plenitude of jewels'	Solar plexus; navel; diaphragm	10	Triangle	Ram	Expansion; heat; sight & color; anus	Rudra old	Lakini	Fire
PSYCHOLOGICAL SIGNIFICANCE: Handles of crucible-triangle form of swastika. Emotion, passions; Rudra is destroyer; affects; belly is action-reaction, no reflection.								
Anahata 'unattackable'	Heart	12	Hexagon	Antelope/gazelle	Movement; touch; feel; penis	Isha	Kakini	Air
PSYCHOLOGICAL SIGNIFICANCE: Conscious. Union of opposites, atman (self) appears. Small flame in castle; heart in lungs. Here is reflection, discrimination, judgment. Come to impersonal aspect of oneself.								
Vishuddha 'purification'	Throat pharyngeal plexus	16	Circle	White elephant	Akasha (space-giving) hearing; mouth	Sada-Shiva	Shakini	Ether
PSYCHOLOGICAL SIGNIFICANCE: Pure concepts, reality of psyche. World is inner drama, has to do with Hindu idea that word and speech beyond tangible reality.								
Ajna 'place of command'	Between the eyes	2	—	None	Manas (mental faculties)	Shambhu	Hakini	None
PSYCHOLOGICAL SIGNIFICANCE: Command, no animal means psychic reality does not require animal, bodily reality. Yogin is a psychic content of God.								
Sahasrara	Above crown on head	1000	Lotus	None	None	None	None	None
PSYCHOLOGICAL SIGNIFICANCE: Shunyata, the void. All being is no longer being. Union of opposites. Advaita (non-two); Nirdvandva (free of opposites), objectless subject. Total union of Shiva-Shakti.								

CHAKRA CHART

CHAKRAS ON THE HUMAN BODY

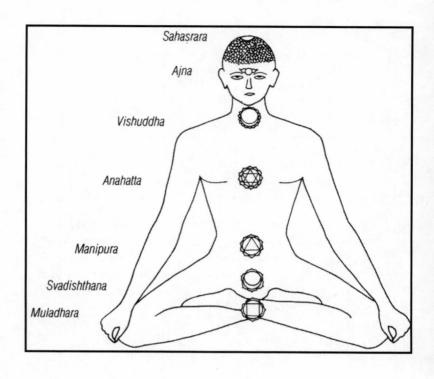

APPENDIX TWO

OCCULT EUGENICS

ISRAEL REGARDIE

Dr. Regardie's article, written sometime in the mid- to late- 1930s, stimulated both of us to pursue his original inspiration. I feel that the reader will strongly benefit from reading between the lines of this article to gain the insights suppressed because of the period in which it was published. Particularly, compare the explicit nature of this work, with the implications hinted at by Dr. Regardie. The power of the methods implied by his works have increased at least a thousand-fold as the cloak of secrecy has been lifted from both normal sexual practices and Tantra. We can be very grateful for the courage Dr. Regardie possessed to write and publish this article. — Christopher S. Hyatt

An automobile manufacturer has already familiarized us with the slogan that "When better cars are built, Whoozis will build them."

With apologies to this manufacturer, may I suggest a variation? "When better babies are born, Occultism will produce them!"

Does this shock you? Does it seem flippant to you? I suppose it does, though I have not intended to be shocking or flippant. But why should this shock you? We are long accustomed to the idea that occultism is not only a philosophy of life and the universe, but what is more important a technique of living and of attainment. Occultism has familiarized us with psychological practices of different kinds, all tending towards the eventual open manifestation of the spiritual faculties of the inner man. Nor is this all. Occultism has also presented us with such concepts as Reincarnation, various grades or types of souls who incarnate on this globe of ours, and the idea of karma determining amongst innumerable other things in what family and in what environment the incoming soul shall live.

What is the purpose of eugenics? Since Mendel's experiments with plants the eugenists believe that by careful breeding we ought to be able to produce a better human stock. A most laudable proposition indeed. They hold that by careful selection of parental types, a higher grade of human intelligence, efficiency and physical health should be possible. Experiments have been conducted extensively with animals. Already it is commonplace that a breed of cattle, for example, may be considerably improved so far as those qualities which their breeders consider important. This being so, it is held that human beings are no exception to this fundamental law of development and growth.

What does occultism have to say on this score? First of all, we find that there is a good deal of objection to the basic scientific postulates. Most important amongst these objections is the widely held belief that human beings in spite of a long anterior line of physical or animal evolution, are not animals. Not being animal but mental or spiritual entities, they are not wholly subject to the physical eugenic laws already observed. This may or may not be so. Who are we to decide? A very great deal more research on chromosomes and genes, especially the mysterious X and Y chromosomes, is necessary before any final opinion can be concluded. Meanwhile, this writer does not believe that scientific explanations by themselves conduce to deep understanding. Always in biology and histology, we are confronted by fundamental questions which are not answerable without at least a mild infiltration of basic occult philosophy. Why the embryo, for example develops as it does is really a very deep mystery. Who can say why at certain set periods limb-buds and sense areas make their appearance? The observed cycle of cell multiplication from the union of sperm and ovum through the morula stage to that of the blastodermic vesicle, requires a very great deal of explaining. Why do cells divide anyway?

How do they come to form a human being? What, to ask a more fundamental question, makes the centrosome split into two? More problems arise as we look deeper. These, however, are beyond my province.

But to return to an earlier philosophic point raised above, we well might argue as follows. If human beings are spiritual beings, and thereby not exclusively subject to purely mechanical laws of heredity, is there a spiritual technique of eugenics as there is a physical technique observed by cattle breeders? To my knowledge this question has not hitherto been raised. What do you think?

Well, there are many points of view. Most prominent is the theosophical one, which is that of most mystico-occult groups. Its argument would run that if two people, prospective parents, lead a pure and holy life according to the lofty ethical teachings and moral schemes laid down by Madame H.P. Blavatsky, and before her by the great spiritual teachers of mankind, then very noble and highly developed souls should be attracted to their sphere when eventually they do decide to have children. Here the emphasis is laid on morals and ethics on the type of life led, rather than on any series of exercises or meditations and practices to be performed. The facts in the case are very helpful. Children of sincere Theosophists and other occult students, as a rule, are not particularly advanced so far as concerns the especial ideals of occultism. Very often they are far less mystically inclined than their parents, to make but little mention of having far less practical ability and capacity than the child issuing from nonmystical families. Of course, the Theosophical explanation in such a case would be the introduction of the Law of Karma. The parents and the child have known each other in past incarnations, and that there are many ties — emotional, mental and physical — which have to be "worked out," to use the cliché so often employed. Old debts on both sides of the ledger have to be paid. And since, often, the parents have no direct conscious knowledge of the karmic stream behind them, and which motivates them, they are therefore at the mercy of life itself or of karma (or the Unconscious) when finally they decide to have children.

This I believe to be the general occult view. It is held not only by Theosophists but by Anthroposophists and other similar groups. However, this philosophy is not especially helpful in enabling men and women deliberately to produce a higher kind of offspring. Nor does it help us in determining the sex of the unborn child — this factor of choice being a very important one.

Prior to embarking upon my thesis, mention ought to be made of Astrology. In this system there is, at least incipiently, a eugenic scheme, in spite of the fact that different astrologers interpret the facts differently. Astrologers will say that certain zodiacal or planetary types would mate well together, whilst other types in marriage would cause each other nothing but pain and unhappiness throughout. As I have said, however, the theory has never been too explicitly developed, certainly not in terms of the kind of children that might be born from such astrological marriage.

In order to ascertain whether new light can be shed upon this factor, I propose to posit as significant a technique which, unfortunately, is only too often sneered at and rejected by the ordinary run of occult students. It is to hypnotism that I refer. I do so deliberately, in spite of the fact that I know that the practice of hypnotism will immediately evoke from certain short-sighted theosophical critics such denunciations as "black magic." These I propose to ignore, reminding them that most assuredly H.P.B. did not condemn hypnotism outright nor its antecedent mesmerism, but she did object to the abuse and malpractice of unscrupulous hypnotists in their misguided experimental work. Some of the experiments performed were, I agree, absolutely damnable and no justification for them is possible. But Blavatsky herself has written "Under what circumstances is hypnotism 'black magic?'" Sufficient to say that whenever the motive which actuates the operator is selfish or detrimental to any living being or beings all such acts are "black magic." Her view was that any suggestion given to a subject having a wrong or evil moral bias is to be abhorred. Suggestions having as their object the determination of whether or not a hypnotized patient would commit crime are to be shunned, her argument being that counter-suggestions may not eradicate the former suggestion from the subject's mind. In which case a positive criminal suggestion has been given which may lie dormant for years, for lives even, but being within the mind as an unconscious entity, it may at some future time or other seek expression.

Since motive, when all is said and done, is assumed to be the determining factor in this matter no real objection can be found to peopling our earth with finer and more highly developed individuals. In fact, William Quan Judge in his *Ocean of Theosophy* points out in connection with the idea of Reincarnation that there are in Devachan some remarkably highly evolved individuals — individuals who unfortunately, have just fallen short of Mahatmaship. The devachanic period between incarnations of these Gnanis, as he calls them is exceedingly lengthy. It is our duty, he states, to provide the right kind of parents and a suitable environment whereby magnetic links can be created which will have the effect of drawing the Gnanis away from their fantastic life in Devachan into a new physical body here on earth. If our motives, then, are to attract such spiritual beings in order to better the earth with the presence of high knowledge, noble wisdom and holy people, surely any blind charge of "black magic" is undeserving of serious attention.

Before proceeding into the heart of my theorem, let me briefly state how it may be possible, for example, to determine in advance the sex of a child. We know from hypnotic experiments that suggestions during hypnotic sleep will produce a very powerful effect both on the mind and body of the patient. Suggestions can be made which will stimulate enormously the imagination of the mother. And imagination is the king faculty of our minds, a magical creative power which is "a potent help in every event of our lives," to quote H.P.B. Assuming, hence, that a young couple had decided that they wished to bless the beauty of their home with a baby, why should it not be an advantage previously to have hypnotized the mother-to-be? Suggestions could be given to her that, when she does conceive, the development of the cells within her womb from the simple cell, through all stages of embryonic life, will produce a male or female child, as their wish may be.

Fantastic? Possibly. Yet, is it any more fantastic than the host of other hypnotic feats that we know definitely to be true and veridical, and about the existence of which we have become complacent? If some argue that the sex of a child is a mechanical affair, determined by the mere accident of which spermatozoon fertilizes a certain ovum, even this argument does not invalidate the hypnotic thesis. We know that mind and the suggestions that mind makes to another mind can produce a powerful effect on the body, and upon the specific parts areas and organs of the body. It is possible to make a suggestion which would affect the sex glands and play an important role in both spermatogenesis and co-genesis. It should be possible therefore, by suggestion, to cause only a spermatozoon bearing X or Y chromosomes, to rise against the ciliary current of the female generative tract to impregnate the appropriate ovum, thus producing an embryo of the particular sex desired. Let me indicate a few of the hypnotic feats already well verified, to show that such an enterprise as I have delineated may not be wholly outside the bounds of possibility.

Delbouef, a Liege psychologist, has recorded innumerable cases of the hypnotization of a servant girl who was not too intelligent. By means of post-hypnotic suggestions, she had calculated unconsciously such arithmetical examples as 11,525 seconds. Under hypnosis, it was suggested to her by Delbouef that 11,525 seconds after she awoke she would make a cross on paper and record the time. She would wake out of the hypnotic sleep completely unaware of the suggestion made, so deeply entranced was she. Some time later she would feel impelled to write. Her Unconscious had calculated the period exactly and made her record it. Moreover, surgical operations have been performed under hypnosis entirely without the use of any anesthetic. The individual experienced no pain, during the removal, for example, of a monstrous scrotal tumor weighing over a hundred weight.

Quite recently, there was recorded in the press a case of painless delivery in childbirth. The mother of five children had been hypnotized some weeks prior to the expected event by her husband who was a psychotherapist. Suggestions had been given that no pain would be experienced. Came the time, labour began, and she was re-hypnotized. The baby was delivered, a healthy girl of eight pounds. During the birth the mother experienced no inconvenience at all, recovering much more quickly than otherwise she would have done.

By suggestion, it is possible to raise on the skin a blister within a few seconds — even as it is possible to remove a blister, likewise by suggestion. Tachycardia, likewise, may be overcome by hardly more than several minutes in the hypnoidal state, whereas low blood pressure and the bodily states which give rise to it will also respond quite rapidly to simple suggestions during hypnosis.

There are thousands of similar cases of cures and other phenomena that are striking and startling but these need not now be mentioned. The interested reader may refer to standard texts and casebooks for these instances. I have simply mentioned these few cases to show what is involved in the discussion. If you reflect upon the mechanism of such bodily changes as have been mentioned above, a great deal of information and insight will have been vouchsafed to you. The smallest physical change produced through the mind by suggestion or by imagination is not less or more miraculous than some vast or unusual bodily change. In any event I am firmly convinced that the determination of sex through the same controlled employment of hypnotism is a logical development of the technique. I should like to see interested parents experiment with it under skilled guidance. At least it should prove more satisfactory and conclusive than the use of bicarbonate of soda, which until recently was employed by some medical men to influence the development of the male sex. One English psychologist to whom I spoke about this some years ago, responded very wittily by saying "Far better an alkaline boy than an acid daughter!"

The really significant question however is this — can we, quite apart from sex, improve the quality of the child? That is to say, can we beforehand arrange that, just as a cow will have certain qualities that render it invaluable to breeders, the child will possess certain mental traits, emotional characteristics and abilities that will make it an asset to the human race? Personally, I believe we can. From a prolonged study of hypnotic phenomena, I am of the opinion that suggestions made at various times during gestation will ensure that only the highest moral qualities will develop in the growing child. Not only so, but if there were prepared on the basis of sound psychology an inventory of the qualities, intellectual and emotional, such a child should have, those qualities could be induced from the conception of the foetus, and manifest themselves in the child as the years went by. Faults and failings could, because of lack of expression and development, be entirely eradicated. Think of what a generation of children we could raise! Contemplate the nature of mankind and the earth if such a policy were definitely and officially inaugurated!

This is but one side of the practical politics. We can go much further by making use of fundamental concepts of Astrology and of certain magical techniques. In a former book of mine *The Art of True Healing* I delineated a simple but very effective technique, based upon some magical practices which were taught to the initiates of the Hermetic Order of the Golden Dawn. In making use of what is known as the Qabalistic Tree of Life, this booklet proposed the concerted employment of colour visualizations and the vibration of names and sounds in order to produce certain psychic effects within both body and mind. Magickal technique as practised within that Order and as described in my books *The Tree of Life* and *The Golden Dawn* [Note: Now expanded into *The Complete Golden Dawn System of Magic,* Falcon Press, 1984. Ed.] could also be suitably employed with a considerable degree of success.

I am certain that a race of geniuses could be developed — geniuses of many different kinds: artistic, scientific and religious. Suppose some parents wished to have a child who was a scientist — a scientist who would assist mankind in its forward march because of his vast scientific knowledge and skill. Astrologically, we could assume that, as a subject, science would be included within the significance of the planet Mercury. The specific type or field of the scientist would be determined by the relation or aspect of some other planet to

Mercury. For the sake of argument, let us assume it to be Jupiter. Now, before conception, let us assume that husband and wife regularly and together practised a series of meditations with the object of filling themselves with the power or vibration of both Mercury and Jupiter. From traditional correspondences we know Orange to be the appropriate colour for Mercury, and the divine Name to be vibrated would be Elohim Tzavoos. Jupiter's colour would be Blue, and its sound value for vibration would be El. The technique I have elsewhere envisaged would be to visualize around these individuals on different occasions a sphere of these colours. On one occasion Orange, on another Blue. Whilst visualizing the sphere, the name is to be constantly vibrated until eventually both felt that these forces are pouring through them, permeating their minds and bodies. Hypnotism could also be included within the curriculum to ensure that a sufficiently deep impression had been made upon both parents. These techniques should be continued even after conception. This will ensure that the vibrations impinge without any possibility of doubt upon the embryo. The results should be that the embryo becomes so permeated by the Mercurial and Jupiterian forces, that after birth its development is psychologically and mechanically conditioned, as it were in a pre-arranged direction. Education, likewise, could be arranged accordingly, to ensure the inevitable development of the capabilities and characteristics already inherent within the child by virtue of these meditations.

Should the parents have aspirations to nurturing a future poet or artist, Venus would be the planetary force to deal with. In this event, as in the case described above, a slight knowledge of ceremonial magic would be no inconsiderable asset. That is to say, if the parents knew how to invoke the required planetary force by means of the appropriate invoking Ritual of the Hexagram and Pentagram, a much closer degree of contact with the desired force could be achieved. These techniques may sound obscure and difficult, I know. In reality they are as simple as they are effectual. The Pentagram Ritual is delineated in my work. [Note: Use the ones in this present book. Ed.], whilst the Hexagram Ritual will be found in *The (Complete) Golden Dawn (System of Magic)* [See the modern version referenced above. Ed.]

To conclude, may I say that this is only the briefest sketch of the possible application of the hypnotic technique. If parents will apply themselves for the sake both of their own children and of humanity, I am profoundly convinced that the results should prove eminently satisfactory. It should be possible to attract from out of Devachan or higher spiritual spheres, high and noble souls whose nature or intrinsic rhythm is of a certain planetary pattern. By embodying their psychological patterns firmly within our own minds via the imagination or by the methods described above, it is conceivable that we should draw them to us, for like attracts itself to like even as love attracts love and hatred inevitably draws hatred. High ideals and motives should likewise attract as though by a magnet similar high ideals and motives, and if our mechanism of operation is adequate, the results also should be commensurate thereto. The difficulty heretofore has been that our methods and techniques have been totally inadequate to our ideals. No doubt the method requires elucidation and more precise application. Experience will provide those details.

THE LESSER BANISHING RITUAL OF THE PENTAGRAM & THE KEYS TO THE MIDDLE PILLAR RITUAL

JOSEPH C. LISIEWSKI, Ph.D.
Adeptus Minor of the Hermetic Order of the Golden Dawn

After having studied Dr. Hyatt's "working guidelines" for performing this ritual, the individual student who is unaware of the dynamics of both the Pentagram and Middle Pillar Ritual will require some additional information concerning the technical aspects and theoretical considerations of these practices. It is as with any new endeavor: understanding must precede proficiency in practice, lest the student waste time and tamper with forces he does not understand. I have been asked to address these areas in order to provide the necessary elements required to facilitate the student's understanding of these ritual actions.

We begin with the theoretical aspects of the Lesser Banishing Ritual of the Pentagram. In this effort, the individual is asked to procure a small, cross-hilt dagger, the blade of which should be no greater than six inches in length. In the study of Magic, this is one of the "Impedimenta", or "Instruments", or "Weapons" of the Art. As with the other Magical Weapons (which do not concern us here), this dagger is a physical representation of a corresponding Psycho-spiritual faculty within the Psyche of the individual; that is, a particular conscious, energetic correlate to the dagger resides within the practitioner.

In this case, the dagger corresponds to the Ruach, or the critical, reasoning, analytical faculty of the mind: in short, the faculty of Reason. Hence, its short length and pointed blade. As reason dispels with a quick, pointed thrust those illogical and confused issues, or that which is unessential to an argument, so too does the dagger dispel those non-essential influences (or entities, as is consistent in Magical practice) not only in the physical area of the student's operation, but in the mental realm as well, through the extension of this faculty symbolized by the dagger through a quick and pointed thrust. Hence, while the practitioner is performing the Banishing Ritual physically in the room in which he will work, he must also perform it in his mind, at the same time. This is really simpler than it sounds, as a little practice will soon illustrate. There is much more Magical Theory at work here; however, our point here is to supply a meaningful insight which will allow the individual to work knowledgeably.

As to the technical aspects, they are principally concerned with the mechanical movements with which the Pentagrams are traced in the air during the physical performance of the ritual. It is absolutely essential, that the Pentagrams be large, and very well proportioned! Dr. Regardie was adamant about this, always reminding me in the beginning of my Magical studies with him, "The larger, the BETTER!"

To proceed, recall that you begin in the East, move to the South, then to the West, next to the North, returning finally to the East. All the Pentagrams are connected to each other by stabbing each in the center with the dagger after tracing it in the air before you, at which point the Divine Name associated with each direction is also vibrated. Then, as you move through each of the "Four Quarters of the World" — as the Qabbalists have termed the four directions — each Pentagram will be connected to the next by a circle, extending from the center of one to the other (as given in the "working guidelines"; you already know the Divine Names to be vibrated in each Quarter). Each Pentagram, and the Circle, are to be visualized in a brilliant blue, blazing light; or if you wish a more romantic description, "aflame with the blue of fire."

Concerning the tracing of the Pentagrams: to trace each, extend your arm such that the dagger is at arms length, and at a position in front of your left knee. With the arm still outstretched, move the dagger upward at a forty-five degree angle, bringing the point of the dagger to rest at a position opposite and just above your head, and in front of you. Next, bring the dagger down, through a forty-five degree angle, to a point opposite your right knee. With your arm still outstretched, sweep through another forty-five degree angle, bringing the dagger to rest at a point opposite your left shoulder; now, sweep a one-hundred and eighty degree angle (a straight line) in front of you to a point opposite your right shoulder. Finally, bring your extended arm with dagger down through a final forty-five degree angle, to connect the first point of the Pentagram, in front of your left knee.

In this way, you have traced a Pentagram of correct proportion which, when vibrated with the Divine Name of each respective Quarter, will "banish" all non-essential entities and influences from your working place. By visualizing the same in your mind as you draw the figures in the air physically, you will also "banish" those non-essential thoughts and feelings which otherwise would impair your operation.

KEYS TO THE MIDDLE PILLAR RITUAL

The technique of the Middle Pillar Ritual which Dr. Hyatt has given in the body of this work, needs little more explanation. Dr. Regardie himself once told this writer that this Ritual was one of the most powerful of all to be found in the subject of Magic, and that it constituted a practice which had enormous spiritual and practical uses for the student. In keeping with his wishes to help the aspirant all that he could, Regardie wrote a very small, almost inconspicuous book entitled, *The Art of True Healing*, published in the 1940s by Helios, in England. The price of it, when I purchased it from the publisher in 1970, was $2.00. The amount of help that I received from the practice of this technique, and its application to my worldly affairs and spiritual growth, is immeasurable. I have found that over the past nineteen years, certain "Keys" if you will, assist the inquirer into the Mysteries to an even greater appreciation of its power, and applicability to his overall condition. Hence, what follows is a brief rendition of those "Keys". They have not only worked for me, but with the large number of students and individuals I have worked with in Magic over the years. It is hoped they will likewise assist the present reader in his search for understanding, and in the control over his own life, and the affairs thereof.

THE KEYS

1. Each Psycho-Bio-Spiritual Center or "Sphere" of activity (which corresponds to a respective site within the physical body) already exists in a state of dynamic activity, and has its own particular "size" i.e., diameter, and volume. When concentrating on each and vibrating the corresponding Divine Name, you are not increasing its activity or its size; rather, you are increasing your conscious awareness of that activity and size. (Note: when using Dr. Hyatt's sexual practices with the Middle Pillar the actual size and activity will in fact change.) The student will find that this knowledge removes his anxiety at attempting to influence the characteristics and dimensions of the spheres.

2. In different sessions, you will note varying sizes of the spheres; particularly, the Coronal (above the head), the Water Center (the sphere formed at the generative organs), and the Earth Center (the sphere formed at your feet). This is as it should be, since the first reflects your devotional mood during a given session, while the latter two reflect your emotional state and the depth of concern over your material affairs.

3. Each Center will elicit an appropriate corresponding physical effect from you, according to its nature. In time, you will also notice a mental effect, which we will not go into here, lest you be subject to suggestion. As to the physical however, you will eventually experience the following: from the Coronal Sphere, a sense of a "crystalline" rotation, directly at the crown of your head; from the Air Center, a diffused coolness;

from the Fire Center, a very distinct rotating ball of heat, extending from the front of your abdomen, to the back of your spine; from the Water Sphere, a rippling, tingling sensation; from the Earth Sphere, a rotating sense of "heaviness."

4. The more proficient you become at making the rhythmic breath completely automatic throughout this ritual, the more powerfully will you feel the Light-Energy called down from the Coronal Sphere passing through your body down the left side, and up the right. This is as it should be. Be careful to note from time to time the condition of the solar plexus: when rhythmic breathing is established, a rippling sensation will be felt over it.

5. When you are scattering the Light-Energy over your body through the "Fountain Technique", your skin will become alive with thousands of tinglings. Again, this is as it should be.

6. Should you work with the various colors of each Sphere as given in *The Art of True Healing,* or *The Complete Golden Dawn System of Magic,* [Falcon Press], and with turning the color of your super-charged aura to the color of the planet being worked with, you will most certainly notice that you shake or quiver, sometimes violently. This is very desirable, as it shows that the energy being called down is truly dissolving those neurotic "blockages" in your psyche, and their corresponding physical centers of body armor. As such, the energy is present for being directed to the specific end which you choose.

7. Expect great ecstasy of the mind when vibrating the Divine Name assigned to the planet and its particular Psychospiritual Center that you are working with. In fact, during your better sessions, you will lose consciousness of all but you and the force being called down.

8. Be certain to draw the super-charged aura within you when the session is ended; take the time to contract it in step with your rhythmic breath, so that in the end it is enclosed by the confines of your physical form.

9. Arise from your Session slowly, stretching your body carefully. You will be amazed to note that you were so wrapped

up in the ritual, that your body feels tight; not a tightness due to tension but rather, from the lack of it. Your body will feel as though it were a "new suit" that must be stretched as it were, before feeling normal again.

10. You will find that when the session is over, you have had a complete loss of the awareness of time. Expect an hour to an hour and a half to have elapsed during the practice. This is an excellent indication that you have truly become absorbed into the ritual. When this happens, your results will be better.

THE TANTRA OF SECTS

Rev. S. Jason Black

"O faithless and perverse generation, how long shall I be with you?"

— Jesus of Nazareth

"So, who the hell's stopping you?"

— The Author

One of the most difficult barriers facing someone who decides to seriously practice some form of Tantrik discipline is the question of religious imagery. Since Tantra is primarily an occult practice, and not a religion, (although the word is attached to a religion in Tibet, and rather hazily to a subset of Hinduism) the object is not worship. But since Tantra has a very strong black magical component, propitiation of presumed (or experienced) spiritual helpers is often required. So also are the use of images and talismans.

This inevitably brings up the question of your religious upbringing. If you are reading this, the odds are that you were raised Jewish or Christian, probably the latter. It cannot be over-emphasized how necessary it is to deal seriously with this, unless you were raised in a totally religion-neutral home. Even then, the pernicious influence can cross generations and, even worse, pervades the entire culture.

My mother's family, to my knowledge, doesn't have a religious bone in their bodies, nor aside from myself and (ugh!) an older cousin who has used her youthful conversion (presumably in her 'twenties) to the Jehovah's Witnesses to terrorize her family for decades, even the younger generation seems devoid of it. And yet, my mother and her four siblings were raised by a fundamentalist Baptist minister and his (probably) paranoid schizophrenic wife. This goon, who died when I was two, would stand on street corners preaching at people while waving his bible, and who, as soon as she was old enough, forced my mother to accompany him, playing a portable foot-peddle organ. Imagine the humiliation this would cause a girl of 13 to 16, especially if she was in an area where her classmates would see her — and she almost certainly was seen.

What has all this to do with our subject? Just this: aside from the schizophrenia — which can be inherited, usually by the same sex — that entire generation, male and female, suffers from extreme forms of disorders common to people raised in, or participating in, Christian fundamentalism. Yet hardly one of them has been involved with a church in my memory. Among other things, from my personal reading and listening to anecdotes, it would not surprise me that as a subgroup, fundamentalist Christians would rank among the very highest in attempted suicide. I *know* from my research that "evangelicals" (which pretty much means the same thing), have admitted with some embarrassment that they rank as the *highest* self-identified group in divorce rate in the United States.

These remarks so far have been addressed primarily to Americans, as Europeans have, by and large, matured beyond this. Still, religious imagery has a hold on our minds that it is difficult to shake. Simple conversion, without extreme and disturbing effort will not do. We have all met (or perhaps are) Wiccans who are essentially Christian in almost all their attitudes, something which would match up with virtually no traditional pagan religion. In addition, I have watched some Crowley groups, several of which I was heavily involved with years ago, slowly, and then with increasing rapidity devolve into a simple New Age church with moral and intellectual stances that would make any Methodist proud. I even attended, about three times, a "Buddhist" group which turned out to be as Christian as the day is long.

Dr. Hyatt remarked, on being told this story, that, unless the group is led by an Oriental raised in the tradition, that is all you will find in this country. In other words, if the leader is some white guy, be prepared for disappointment. Dr. Hyatt and I have one friend, now a Theravedic Buddhist monk, who seems to have well and truly made the switch. But this fellow, whom we originally met in Crowleyan magic, was an unusually serious, extreme sort, who actually went to India and meditated in a burning ground, his body smeared with ashes.

As I have repeated until blue in the face, both magic and Tantrism involve physical practice, not just mental hijinks of one kind or another. It has been an urban myth at least since the early seventies that spirits are "just" created from your imagination. Anyone who has experienced poltergeist phenomena knows better. I have seen more than one practitioner, who, having called up something he thought was supposed to be his imaginary friend, hightail it for the nearest bible study group when his expectations were exceeded. I have simply stopped wasting my time telling people into Wicca or Crowley to read volumes on psychic research. In India, a year or so before this writing, a man — the patriarch of a family of Kali worshipers — was arrested for the machete murder of most of his family. His defense was that he was possessed during a worship ceremony (a common occurrence) and had no memory of the event. Moreover, of course, *he* didn't do it. The surviving family members confirmed this. This was reported in the American media as an item of black humor ("them wacky furriners. They should know Jayzus.") with no follow-up on the result of his trial that I have seen.

This misunderstanding can be laid at the door first, of Aleister Crowley (in his introduction to *The Goetia*) and secondly to Dr. Carl Jung — now used, primarily by Wiccans, but with plenty to go around — to make communication by and with spirits seem acceptable in modern terms. It is *not* acceptable in modern terms, nor are most of the important assertions of Tantrik philosophy in general. The practitioner of any serious path of occult self-development must face up to just what extent the society (especially American) is his enemy, and behave accordingly. The constitution that he has never read will not stop your neighbor from breaking into your house, or attacking you as you step out of it. You may find also, that nothing could interest the police less than the report of a crime prompted by a local church. Religious crime remains one of the great unreported crimes in America. Unreported, that is, by the police, who, if they deal with it at all, call it something else. Nothing less than multiple witnesses or security video will do. I point this out because "neo-pagans" remain remarkably innocent on the subject, but also because, if you take the care to hide your activities anyway, the more serious ones, that is, it will free you for more effective practice.

Tantrism is a body of technique attached generally to two very different Oriental religions. Yet there are also Tantrik practices under other names in Taoism and Islam (although you wouldn't know it lately). So, which religion does it belong to? Clearly, no single one. The technique is what is important. In Taoism, which of course is the foundation of almost all oriental magic outside Islamic countries, there is the practice of "alchemy" — which is the English translation of a Chinese term that does not translate as alchemy. It is, in fact, Tantrik yoga, replete with the manipulation of kundalini and sexual yoga, with sexual vampirism as an important component. It has been widely suggested that Tantra is "goddess-worship" (no such worship is involved in Taoist yoga or, certainly, in Islamic Sufism) thus being embraced by Wiccans for propaganda purposes if for no other. Yet most (not exactly all) Wiccans loudly denounce blood sacrifice — and the divine patronesses of Tantriks in the East have altars that drip with blood. Interestingly, it was once supposed that the majority of people attracted to Wicca and organizations like Crowley's O.T.O., came from a rejected Catholic background, hence a fondness for ceremony not present in the average Protestant. In close to thirty years of active involvement with hard-core occult groups, I suspect that nothing could be further from the truth. Almost every "neo-pagan" that I have ever met has come from a Protestant — frequently fundamentalist — background. (For the record, in spite of the story I told about one side of my family, I do not come from a fundamentalist church, but went to a liberal Presbyterian church until I refused to go anymore at the age of 14.)

The point is, that people who *do* come from such a place psychologically, can have devastating relapses. An example that reached national attention, although definitely *not* slanted in the way that I'm going to, is the story of the death of Cassie Bernall. She was a high school student at Columbine High School in Colorado. She had gotten into Wicca, whether in a group, or only through books I do not know, since I have not read the "biography" put out posthumously by a Christian press. For those who don't know, Columbine is a hop and a skip away from Colorado Springs, dubbed "the Evangelical Vatican." Her parents, whose denomination is unknown to me, were deeply disturbed by this "dark" turn in her interests.

Don't say it.

They conferred with some friends who had their child accompany Cassie to a fundamentalist...er...evangelical camp. I seem to recall that this lasted for a good week so it may have been during summer vacation. At any rate, brainwashing takes time, even with a high school girl. She returned home a raving fundamentalist. Some time later, two boys, tormented throughout their lives by fellow "Christian" students and ignored by the traditionally mediocre faculty, walk into the school armed with pistols, rifles and bombs, and begin killing people. On a stroll through the library, they asked "Does anyone here believe in God?" and Cassie, full of the holy spirit, stood up, smiled, and said: "Yes, I do." Boom goes her face. I leave it to the reader to decide if there were others involved in her death besides the shooter.

There are several rules, that, from years of practice, I think the seeker should follow:

1. Pay close attention to phenomena, not theology. Tantra, in spite of what the Dali Lama says, is amoral. The sun may be the center of the solar system, but in serious esoteric practice, *the center of the universe is you*. Morality is a collection

of rules not defended by reason, whereas ethical behavior is essentially self-defensive. In Hindu Tantra, divesting yourself of the bonds of Karma involves the elimination of guilt. In that culture, this has involved the calculated committing of crime, as opposed to crime for profit or that which is done in the name of a religious or political hierarchy.

2. Any imagery used on an altar or for meditation should be a desecration of that of the religion you were raised in. For Protestant sects (excepting Episcopalians) this might be difficult, so Catholic imagery should be used if you were Christian, since our pop culture is suffused with it. Please refer to *The Exorcist*, or *Satanic Rites of Dracula*. Or a Dennis Wheatly novel. This most emphatically applies to the reader who thinks he or she is a neo-pagan. Nazi imagery is always useful (especially for Jews) in Western Tantrik practice. The swastika is a link between Eastern religions and the West, and many of you may be familiar with the strange alliance between Tibet and the Third Reich. (Himmler even began an official S.S. program of sex magic in ancient graveyards to reincarnate the souls of aryan warriors.) This is one of the few symbols that are useful even for actual Nazis since, generally speaking, it is a symbol that one tends to hide. Except, that is, on your mantelpiece in Berlin. Dr. Hyatt and I once constructed an All Hallow's Eve altar with inverted crosses decorated with swastikas in the center. That would cover it for almost everyone. I once performed a ritual while playing a movie about the crucifixion with the sound off. Gibson's *The Passion of the Christ* will prove highly useful.

3. If you use ceremonial magic, find a traditional grimoire; or, in the case of Afro-Caribbean magic, a formulary the instructions of which you have the wherewithal to follow, *and follow them*. They are *not* diversions for the uninitiated. Another modern myth. This cannot be emphasized enough. If, that is, you find it useful to use evocation in connection with Tantrik practice.

4. If you are comfortable with what is on your altar or in your journals, enough to feel at ease with someone other than a fellow practitioner seeing them in or out of your presence,

you have done it wrong. Do not trust your family or neighbors.

5. Do not use images, symbols, or texts that do not scare the shit out of you on some level. This will be among the most difficult thing to do at times. Also, do not hesitate to use pop culture images for meditation. If you engage in sexual activity during the course of your efforts it is not necessary or even desirable for them to be aware of it for the experiment to be successful. Crowley amply describes this in his diaries, and I know it myself from past experience. While the partners in this practice can be lovers, any suggestion that they must be is a flat betrayal of Tantrik tradition. Please remember also, that Tantra is not about sex. That is just another myth. It is about freedom from programming first, and power second.

6. Do not ignore your environment. You are not in ninth century India. For Christians, considering the world situation, the Book of Revelation would be an appropriate text to recite or read from, as would Crowley's *Book of the Law*, since his entire theology is based on Revelation. For Jews, I recommend the Book of Daniel, and the Book of Enoch. Nephilim fucking is always useful in the work.

7. Go to confession, and confess to things you didn't do. Don't tell them the ones you did.

APPENDIX FIVE

TANTRA & TEEN IDOLS
SHIVA & SHAKTI IN POPULAR ART

S. JASON BLACK

About two years ago I attended a concert performance of a major rock band at a beautiful open-air amphitheater in Southern California. It was my birthday, and I had been partying late the night before, with the not-unexpected result that I was more than a little ill when I arrived at the venue. As a result I was worried that the experience would be spoiled for me. Rather unusually, the band's set began with a loud, long drum solo. This had the effect of causing a companion to plug his ears, but it threw me into a trance that continued to deepen as the music continued.

When the solo ended, I came out of it to find a worried expression on my friend's face, and all my symptoms — nausea, headache and sleepiness — completely vanished.

When asked why the alarmed look, my friend told me that he had tried to talk to me several times during the interlude, and had gotten no response. He began to think that I was either drugged or seriously ill. I was able to enjoy the entirety of the concert — and the evening afterward — with renewed energy and a pervasive feeling of well-being.

This is one of the few experiences I have had at such an affair which border on transcendental. Since I have extensive experience of hypnosis and deep meditational states (which I continue to use on an almost daily basis), I want to be clear that I use the word "trance" in a clinical, not a slang, context.

There has been some controversy over what, exactly, constitutes Tantrik technique. Some writers identify it as religion, and yet there are Hindu and Buddhist Tantras with essentially similar techniques and goals. Many of the more heretical Sufi practices also seem to have a Tantrik origin, but they avoid the label because the basic ideas behind Tantra are contrary to Islamic ideology, as they are to that of Judaism and Christianity (in their accepted forms at least).

Taoism, which has given us the *I Ching* and a concise form of sexual alchemy, is the oldest system to openly use Tantrik techniques, though the techniques themselves go back to prehistoric shamanism, or to lost Atlantis, depending who you believe.

My own experience at the concert described above was a classic example of mild but authentic shamanic healing, still an intrinsic part of Tibetan practice

As this book has made clear, Tantrik techniques consist of a combination of *physical practices* and magical or metaphysical assumptions about the world. The strong emphasis on human biology and instinct is what distinguishes Tantra most deeply from what many people think of as magical tradition, and what removes it from religious tradition as well. This last is due to the fact that the principle goal of Tantrik practice is (in modern terms) to de-program the student from the inhibitions, limitations and beliefs instilled by parent, church and state. This is not calculated to win approval from orthodox organizations whose main function is social control.

After this process of de-programming is well under way, a program of new learning is begun, in which the student ultimately seeks the development of magical powers over the world and himself (here it differs from orthodox Buddhism) and to achieve the greatest degree of physical perfection of which he is capable. In the Orient, this semi-secret stratum of belief and practice appears in the arts and popular beliefs in spite of official disapproval. I began asking myself if a similar subtle influence can be seen in the West, now, a century after the beginning of the "magical revival." I believe the answer is "yes."

My interest in Tantra was originally sparked by my study of European magic, especially some of the forms espoused by Aleister Crowley. I lived in Hollywood at the time and frequented the many music clubs there. As time passed, I became struck by what seemed to be genuine mystical or occult undercurrents to what I was seeing. Much of this was unconscious on the part of performers and participants, but some, I was to find, was quite deliberate.

My eye was first caught by image. In both local publicity and slick national publications I noticed a combination of eroticism and iconography that reminded me of the depiction's of gods and bodhisattvas in the East. Some even reminded me of specific deities; the bass player, Nikki Sixx, for example, has always reminded me of Shiva.

The involvement of guitarist Jimmy Page with the occult is well-known and the "satanic" posing of the Rolling Stones has become part of musical folklore. What is less obvious, because less intentional, is the creation of what — to a Hindu — would be a divine avatar from a well-known artist.

I say "creation" but, in fact, these things seem to happen spontaneously and unexpectedly, though to be sure, every attempt is made to orchestrate the phenomenon after it occurs.

This is not unique to the twentieth century. The nineteenth-century Romantic movement seems to have seen the first artists "worshipped" by a huge public. These include the composer and pianist Franz Liszt; the violinist Pagannini (who was rumored to have made a demonic pact); and of course, Lord Byron, the archetype of all of them.

Our century though, seems to have had a virtual explosion of these people, for some of whom it was a devastating experience.

The early 70's teen idol David Cassidy seems to have fit the pattern I'm thinking of better than most. According to the story told in his recent autobiography *Come On, Get Happy; Fear and Loathing On The Partridge Family Bus,* he was inundated with a wave of hysterical sexual attention totally unprecedented up to that time, even by Elvis. Both he and his studio were taken aback, but they rushed to try to control — and profit from — the situation. It wasn't so much his performing talents that won the attention (he was very professional, but most of what he did was outside his control) but a strange gestalt of appearance, personality and timing that created a furor that hasn't really been repeated since. That, and his reputedly remarkable penis size makes his life story seem weirdly like a version of the story of Krishna.

The endless work hours, legal wrangling, and constant harassment (worship?) eventually caused a collapse. An interesting part of the whole phenomenon is the complete lack of interest this passionate obsession can devolve into, almost a kind of psychic death. For those cynics who assume all such phenomena are created by publicity, I would like to point out that the national fan magazines have tried and failed to repeat such a gold mine in the twenty-five years since. In a recent article on the publishing industry I read that several of the perennial fan magazines were even in trouble financially as a result.

In some of the early Gnostic versions of the Jesus myth, the Christ-spirit entered Jesus at the age of thirty, and left him at thirty-three; thus, in their eyes, the incarnation was an act of possession, not "the word made flesh." The person of Jesus himself was thus irrelevant.

Speaking of penis size, another priapic figure of legend in the music world is Iggy Pop. His blatant sexuality (getting the occasional blow-job on stage) and deliberate defiance of both the public and his audiences' sensibilities, should earn him Tantrik sainthood. Unlike Mr. Cassidy, Iggy Pop has sometimes given the impression that his performance style was deliberately esoteric. He has publicly described himself as a "Dionysian" performer and his frequent drug intoxication and athletic dancing while performing are both sacred to Shiva. At various points in his career he was known for the wearing of body paint, cross-dressing and even self-mutilation — all practices of both shamanism and the extreme Left-Hand Tantrik sects.

I would mention Jim Morrison here, but his "shamanization" has become such a cottage industry that all that can be said has surely already been said.

In the area of film, the late Bruce Lee brought a popular interest in the martial arts to the West. While not a follower of Tantra *per se,* his writing shows that he was heavily influenced by Taoism and some scholars think that Zen — from which so many of the martial arts come — may have Tantrik roots. It should be pointed out that far from vulgarizing his vocation, Lee was following in a very old Shaolin tradition of showmanship. For centuries they were known for the public acrobatic performances of their adepts and their participation in parades.

I have spent most of my time commenting on performers, since in many ways they are the most visible examples, but other areas as well show this esoteric influence.

Since their explosion of popularity in the early sixties, comic books and various other kinds of graphic storytelling media have acquired an adult audience in the United States. This has been the case much longer in Europe, and especially, in Japan. Even at the beginning, the creators of comic characters drew on the arcana of magic and of the Far East for subject matter. I can remember, as a child, discovering the stories of Dr. Strange, then still being done by his creator, the legendary cartoonist Steve Ditko. Dr. Strange was a wealthy, materialistic surgeon whose life collapsed, thus sending him in desperation to Tibet in search of meaning. There, in chelaship to an ancient lama, he learns the arts of magic. While wildly simplified and exaggerated for its target audience, I later realized that the Dr. Strange stories were based on a certain amount of solid tradition.

More recently, for the adult market, there have been several characters, sometimes in limited series, that openly gain their power from Tantrik practices. The material in some of these is not nearly so fanciful and based on solid research by their creators. A particularly compelling example of this is *The Adventures of Luther Arkwright* (collected in three volumes by Proutt Publications in 1989) by the incredibly talented Bryan Talbot. This wonderful piece of work combines science fiction, multi-universe theory and a sophisticated treatment of Tantrik techniques of psychic development. Thanks to the

wider market and loosening of censorship, the sexual aspects
of Tantrism are dealt with openly.

Some interesting hybrids have developed from this current
as well. Genesis P-Orridge and Thee Temple ov Psykick Youth
in Britain use a combination of music, graphic art, video and
eroticism as well as the written word to deliberately spread
the philosophy of Aleister Crowley and the Tantrik magicians.

Some of my comparisons here may initially strike the
reader as frivolous, but I intend them quite seriously. Just as
the techniques of ceremonial magic are the same the world
over, so is the Tantrik strain of self-development a part of
man's natural heritage. Every culture has divine avatars
whether they are prepared to acknowledge them or not. And
the Western world, with the decline of Christianity from
political power to crackpotism which we now see, may at last
be recovering what it had lost for so long. The signs are right
in front of us.

APPENDIX SIX

RIDING THE SERPENT
ASPECTS OF PRACTICAL SEXUAL MAGIC

PHIL HINE

This essay outlines the practical applications of sexual magic in terms of five functional areas of technique: Sorcery, Divination, Invocation, Evocation and Illumination. Since most magical theories and 'explanations' of sex-magic are at best, arbitrary, I have eschewed any discussion of these in favor of describing practical techniques.

BASIC APPROACHES

To begin, I will examine some areas of magical development and preparation which, in my opinion, need delving into as one becomes seriously concerned with magical work. They are termed 'basic' approaches as I feel that they are the areas which, once work on them has begun, will continue to be foundations of your magical experience. Where relevant, I will discuss these areas in the context of sexual magic, but it should be borne in mind that these areas are applicable to *all* aspects of magical work.

RELAXATION

The ability to relax is of central importance in modern magical practice, yet it is all too easily forgotten or relegated to something which is done for a few minutes before a ritual. When we relax, we are taking ourselves out of the 'what-if?...look at that...I wish I hadn't said that... But...phwoarr!' inner-world of self-reflection, self-conversations, and suppositions that

176

continually projects back into our past and forward into our futures, both immediate and imagined. When we relax, we are aware of the immediate present, of our physical presence and our immediate environment. If we are relaxed, then we can be attentive to what is happening, rather than what we *think* is happening, or what we would *like* to be happening. In learning to relax, we are causing, at a very basic level, a change in our reality in accordance with will — via the union of desire, imagination and breathing.

Relaxation not only has physiological benefits, but also can lead eventually to quite startling changes in how we view ourselves and others. If we can learn to relax and enjoy a situation, particularly one that is novel or unfamiliar, then we are much more likely to be open to surprises and changes, rather than superimposing one set of possibilities onto it. Relaxation is particularly important when it comes to sexual magic. Relaxation techniques can help you learn about your physical presence — the wisdom of your own flesh.

INTUITION & SELF-TRUST

There is much mystical woffling about the development of the intuition, but it is important that you trust your own feelings about someone or something. We often 'go along' with other people for fear of upsetting them or 'losing' them, but in doing so, we devalue what we ourselves want, and subordinate it to what we think are the desires of others. If you've ever found yourself having sex with someone in order to 'keep the peace', then you should know what I mean here.

Another strand in this process is the recovery of love from it's imprisonment in consumer-romanticism. Western ideas of love have become commodified to the extent that the language of desire is largely the language of ownership. Science Fiction Novelist Samuel R. Delaney puts it thus:

> "*She or he who desires, listens. She or he who is desired, speaks.*"

Love bound by rules, duties, morals and projected in media memes serves to maintain alienation between individuals, driving the wedge between self and other, thought and flesh. In attempting to grow beyond one's cultural conditioning it is important to treat all commonly-held beliefs with deep suspicion, yet with an overwhelming optimism and confidence that will carry you through your darkest hours.

INTIMACY & TRANSFORMATION

Intimacy thrives in an atmosphere of trust and respect on all sides. Close intimacy can develop between members of a group without ever manifesting as partner-swapping or group sex. In my experience, intimacy is all the stronger between individuals when sex is no longer an issue. A friend put it to me in this way: "You can have friends, or lovers, but rarely people who are both at the same time." Research by psychologists into the experience of intimacy has concluded that the degree of intimacy that a person experiences is related to the degree of expression, awareness, and interpersonal contact that is experienced during sex. Mosher (1980) created a typology of three levels of intimacy: Ego-Centered, Surface-Centered, and Core-Centered. If one is predominantly Ego-Centered, then one is only concerned with one's own immediate gratification — any partners are considered only as instruments for the fulfillment of physical or status needs. Surface-Centered involvement reflects a major concern with sexual 'performance' and pleasure, for self and partners. Core-centered involvement however, is the willingness to open oneself fully to one's partners, and is associated with 'peak' gnoses characterized by the experience of loss of ego-boundary, or oceanic body-bliss which appears as a contact with something 'beyond' oneself.

SUBTLE BODY MAPS

Another element of occult theory relating to sexual magic are the various maps available of the subtle body — the most-quoted being the chakra system which virtually every modern book on Sexual Magic seems to contain. Like the aura, chakras have become so much a part of the Western esoteric belief-system that their validity is hardly ever questioned. There is much written about awakening one's chakras, and the originally Tantric metaphor has been pulled around so that it fits in with Jungian ideas or Qabalah, depending on the bent of the particular author. My own perspective is that you don't *need* to know anything about or do anything with subtle body maps such as the chakra system in order to do sex-magic. You can of course, use them *if you want to,* but they are by no means essential.

SORCERY

The use of sexual stimulation for Sorcery or Results Magic has been popularized, at least in the general counter-culture by the now-defunct Temple of Psychic Youth. TOPY projects such as "The Sigils Book" and "The Gray Book" stressed the simple, yet highly effective technique of sigil magic, powered by magical (i.e., intentional) masturbation. The use of self-pleasuring for acts of sorcery is well-documented in the magical diaries of contemporary magicians such as Aleister Crowley, Leah Hirsig, and Austin Osman Spare. The majority of sexual magic workings recorded by Aleister Crowley seem to have been for money, fascination, success, youth and magical energy. Crowley also used sexual fluids ('elixir') in order to consecrate talismans and charms.

If you are serious about practicing sexual magic, then being practiced at self-pleasuring is almost a prime requisite. Prolonged self-pleasuring is a wonderful way of entering various shades of Erotognosis, in all types of sex-magic operations. This may well seem to be a let-down for anyone who is hoping to use the 'pose' of being a magician in order to get laid, or is hoping to find the wild orgiastic rites dreamed up by the 'yellow press', but it is possible (and often more desirable) to pursue all aspects of sexual magic as solo workings.

A first step though, is to overcome any guilt feelings which hover around the subject of self-pleasure, for example, feelings that it is somehow 'dirty' or a sign of inadequacy. The ability to give yourself pleasure is a key-indicator of self-love and relaxation. Magical Masturbation however, is also a way of discovering the 'wisdom of your flesh'. Whilst masturbating you can focus awareness upon your breathing, on which muscle groups tense at what point, on which pleasure-points enhance your sensations, on shifts in body posture, and, by 'leaning into' your pleasure, how to prolong it. Obviously, the more you are able to experience pleasure, and the better your contact with your own flesh, the more useful and effective you will find sex-magic techniques.

DIVINATION

When we turn to acts of divination, the most effective use of sexual stimulation is to promote a state of consciousness in a participant who is designated as a central focus, or 'vehicle' for an oracular transmission. Sensual stimulation can be very effective in generating the ambiance that allows one to slip progressively into an Oracular trance. Like any other aspect of sexual magic, the effect you obtain very much depends on how you set things up. Oracular trance may result as a result of either frenzy or lassitude. The latter may begin with prolonged immersion in a hot bath which has been laced with expensive unguents. This has the dual effect of being both relaxing and tiring. The bath also acts as the 'banishing' marking the passage of the oracular vehicle from the normal to the superlucent. The oracle is attended upon in his or her bath, and then lifted from it, dried and perfumed. The oracle is taken to the place where the oracular rite is to be set (preferably a heated room) and is seated comfortably. From this point in, the oracular vehicle is regarded as a priest or priestess, and has all their needs attended to by other celebrants. The oracular lassitude may be heightened by massage, light stroking, or oral stimulation.

A second option for divination might be the 'reading' of splatterings of semen against a suitable medium. This would require a talent in free-form divination techniques such as reading tea-leaves. The degree of erotognosis may be intensified by stimulation (by oneself or 'assistants') which continues after ejaculation has taken place. An analogous technique for female magicians is the soaking of patches of cloth with menstrual blood, in order to form figures which can be used in the manner of Rorschach blots.

INVOCATION

The practice of Invocation is one of the most commonly-used magical techniques, involving using various sensory aids (i.e., voice, gesture, posture, smell) in order that you, or another person, may identify as completely as possible with the character of an entity — usually (but not exclusively) a mythological goddess or god. This practice results in various shades of trance, the two poles of which are known as Overshadowing and Possession. In Overshadowing, the recipient remains self-aware, with altered perceptions, whilst in possession, the recipient's identity is seemingly submerged by that of the invoked entity, and the individual may be able to demonstrate abilities related to that mythic character with no ill-effects. The purpose of invocation is to either invoke into yourself the power of an entity, so that you may, by identification with the entity, direct that power, or, by invoking onto another person, petition a deity directly, or experience it's power through another. The power of a human being possessed or ridden by a god can create a powerful presence, which may become the focus of ritual or free-form ecstatica.

In acts of invocation, excess of stimuli is almost mandatory. Thus one could begin an invocationary rite by spending a few days behaving in such a manner as might be pleasing to the character one aims to invoke. Daily meditation upon the qualities of the subject of one's invocation could be reinforced by the presence of appropriate colors, scents, sacred objects, food and clothes. In sex-magic invocation the aim is the infusion of divine frenzy in the union of human and super-human through the medium of the flesh. The means by which a sex-magic invocation proceeds depends upon the character being invoked, the number of participants, and the purpose of the invocation, which may range from asking the god or goddess to confer knowledge, inspiration, or a particular power, to oracular pronouncements from the god or goddess. The 'power' of the entity so invoked may also be used to sanctify ritual objects and magical weapons through the touch of the manifested deity or application of it's hosts sexual fluids.

If you are intending to use sexually-oriented rites in order to invoke a particular god or goddess, please be sure that you choose the appropriate method by which to please the entity in question. For example, whilst rites involving flagellation or masturbation are eminently suitable for Pan, Artemis, from what we know of her character, would probably find such activities entirely inappropriate!

EVOCATION

Evocation is the practice of 'calling forth an entity' for the purpose of forming a relationship with it. This form of magic tends to be associated with the creation of Servitors or thought-forms, and the conjuration of spirits from grimoires such as *The Key of Solomon The King*. The use of sexual magic in an evocatory mode is particularly concerned with entities known as Succubi (from the Latin, "to lie under") and Incubi (Latin: "to lie upon"), or Servitors projected by sex-magic evocation. The following essay combines both approaches.

Cacodemonic Copulations

The subject of Incubi and Succubi and their visitations is rarely dealt with by modern magical writers, although they have been used time and time again by various hacks of the horror genre. Sex-Demons have been banished — either explained away as hallucination or junked as a product of Christian masturbatory mythos. Any occultists this side of the twentieth-century that do mention them, usually do so in the context of warning against traffic with such entities, believing that the dangers of loss of vitality or obsession is the inevitable result. Again this is very much a 'Western' view of the matter. In Japanese magical mythology, phantom lovers are known as fox maidens, and it was considered lucky for a man to be visited by one.

According to William S. Burroughs, people's attitudes towards these beings may change, but such visitations are probably more frequent than most people suppose. He classes them as a type of familiar and notes that, like animal or elemental familiars, they are dependent on a relationship with a human host for their own development. Similar ideas can be found in the Kaula school of Tantrika, where there are rites for contacting such beings, who will perform tasks for the magician if they are sacrificially offered 'sexual energy'.

So How Do You Go About Acquiring a Demon Lover?

The Liminal Gnosis

Playing with such entities generally falls into the class of magical technique known as Evocation, and a form of Gnosis which is often the most effective is the so-called Liminal state, when one is half-asleep, half-awake. The body is completely relaxed, either from a relaxation exercise, or physical exhaustion; yet the mind is clear, and you simply allow images and sounds to arise before you. If you can learn to enter and prolong this state, then it is very useful for scrying, dream control or virtual (astral) explorations.

Erotic Evocation

To prepare for the Evocation of a Demon Lover, seek to inflame yourself through all possible modes of sensory stimulation — books, films, pornographic material, the diffusion of perfumes that have erotic association, body massage, masturbation without orgasm — any technique which serves to heighten your sexual arousal globally — that is, without being directed to any particular individual (real or imaginary).

The Evocatory scenario is a progression of intense sessions which may begin as follows:

1. Lie naked on your bed, the room in darkness, but for the glow of a single candle. You have bathed and relaxed yourself. Seductive perfumes are diffused throughout the room and you have prepared the space as though you are about to receive a lover. Slowly, begin to caress yourself, intensely feeling each touch, each shiver of pleasure; imagining that the touch comes from an invisible lover who hovers above you. Concentrate at first on secondary erogenous zones when inflaming yourself, and stay as relaxed as possible. Any

significant dream-images that follow such a session should be recorded.

2. Repeat this experience, gradually allowing yourself to become increasingly excited, and slowly visualize the build-up of a shadowy form — fingers, lips, breast, thighs — parts of the lovers body which come into fleeting contact with your own. As you repeat the experience, associations will form between sensory stimuli and it can be helpful if you can create a special scent which, while having erotic associations, is unique for this operation. You should also take care to note any particular body postures and gestures (caresses) that you find yourself making — these can act as sensual asanas and mudras for the operation.

3. The final session of this sequence proceeds as above, but *slowly* allow yourself to approach orgasm. If you are experienced enough, and in touch with your body enough to allow yourself to hover on the brink of orgasm for as long as possible, then so much the better. As you approach orgasm, begin to vocalize love-noises, letting these sounds become glossolalia — until a distinct sound (it may or may not be an actual word) begins to repeat itself through you. As you attain orgasm, project this sound into the shadow-form above you, and see the shadow-form becoming distinct and clear. You may find that details of the entity which have been hitherto indistinct, will become clear in the illuminating flashes of orgasm. Sexual fluids released in this working can form the basis of a material sigil, but this is optional.

Now That You've Evoked Me Here, What Are We Going To Do?

Having gone through the process of evoking a Demon Lover, what can you actually do with them? The first point to consider is the states in which interaction with the entity takes place. What little magical writing there is on the subject tends to concentrate on Dream Magick, but it is also possible to continue using the Liminal Gnosis and, an often-undervalued area of magick, Working with Mirrors. There is also the possibility of Invocatory work with Demon Lovers.

Dream Yoga

Once you have evoked your demon lover, you can choose to interact with it through dreams. One of the easiest techniques of Dream Control is to use a sigil. Since I'm sure most people are familiar with the basics of Sigil Magick, I will merely draw your attention to the point that a sigil need not be either a glyph or mantra, but can also take the form of a scent, or sequence of images. You can use earlier practice in the Liminal Gnosis to launch a sigil to meet your Demon Lover in your dreams. You could even try and key the appearance of the entity to the triggering of a Lucid Dream.

Liminal Gnosis

If your earlier practice has been successful, you will already have some experience of the Liminal Gnosis. Sexual Arousal is but one of the entry-routes into this state, and you might try and find other routes. Interaction with the Demon-Lover can be made in this state, and you might find here that you get dreams which follow-through the encounter.

Mirror-Magick

The Liminal Gnosis can be enhanced by the use of a mirror. The use of reflective surfaces for interacting with entities has a long and venerable history, ranging from shamanic practices among the Maori, Pawnee and Nkomis of Africa, to the explorations of Dr. John Dee. Demon-Lovers may be summoned into a mirror, where they may be cross-examined. A cautionary note here is that Dr. Dee made the claim that from time to time, one of the spirits he contacted — a young girl called Midimi — would emerge from his scrying crystal and cavort about his study This could have interesting possibilities when working with a Demon Lover!

Whichever states you choose to explore, the next consideration is of course, what you are going to do. Well, the very act of experimenting with this approach should in itself be instructive, and at the very least, enjoyable. However, the following applications for Demon Lover work include:

1. Enchantment: Here, you are basically forming a Pact with the entity — using it as you would use any other kind of Sorcery Servitor — you fuck it and it carries out its assigned task (which is not necessarily confined to the sphere of sexuality). One technique is to seed the entity with a sigil, which will gestate within the body of the entity, in a similar manner to a wishing box.

2. Illumination: According to Austin Osman Spare, desires are spirits that wish to incarnate. You can deploy a Demon Lover to assist you with the formulation of an Alphabet of Desire, wherein each sacred letter can become a sex-demon in itself, to be used in acts of self-exploration and self-modification. Your Demon Lover can assist you in recognizing, binding, and integrating the hidden demons of your psyche which relate to sexuality and other primal drives.

3. Divination: Divinatory applications include dream-oracles, or flash-gnoses which may extend into the waking state. You may find, for example, that, following a request for a dream-oracle, your demon lover only gives you half the key, as it were. The other half is waiting in the waking world — some incident that sparks a moment of gnosis in which you realize the link between thought/emotion and some physical object or situation. Oracles are rarely straight-forwards.

4. Invocation: Traditional magical theory (such as it is) tends to frown on invoking entities such as Demon Lovers, as they are not considered to have enough of a developed persona to make it worthwhile. However, long-term magical use of such an entity does tend to build up the appearance of an independent persona, particularly if you make careful note of any quirks, personality traits, or mannerisms that the entity seems to be displaying. I see no reason why, at some stage, you shouldn't try invocatory work with a Demon Lover. It could be instructive, if only for shifting latent sexual selves into the directors chair of the Ego.

A Word of Warning

The practice of intercourse with Demon Lovers is not without its dangers. The most obvious of these is obsession. In its broadest sense, obsession is the term we apply to a situation where the magician has relinquished will to an entity (usually of his own creation). Obsessions with a sexual component are particularly difficult to deal with — anyone who has had an obsessional crush on someone else will know what I mean. Sex, like anything else, can become an addiction which erodes the will. Intercourse with Demon Lovers is no exception, so self-discipline at all times, is important. Although a Demon Lover can generate a great deal of fascination and erotic tension, this should only be employed as a source of gnosis and magical work, and not allowed to get out of control. It can be useful to only use the entity for specific projects, and then, at staggered intervals. Intercourse with these entities *can* be exhausting. This is not so much due to any vampiric quality on their part, but is related to working in unusual states of consciousness — similar problems arise with extended astral, dream, or liminal work.

Another problem relating to this work is also fairly obvious — that the Demon Lover becomes a substitute for a physical partner. As with any relationship between human and entity (be it demon or deity), it is useful to assume its independent existence — if only during the interaction. However, I have seen warnings in a variety of magical grade papers that hint of the dire consequences of giving these entities the same regard that you would a human lover. By the same token, conjuring a Demon Lover for the precise reason that you lack a human lover is tantamount to inviting obsession, with all the attendant problems. As success with this technique requires an appreciation of your own sensuality, bodily awareness, sexual feelings and orgasmic response, it should not be attempted by the overly frustrated, or the sexually inept or inexperienced.

This practice should also lead to a wider appreciation of your sexual being and possible range of sexual identities. If you have sealed disturbing elements of your sexuality behind blocks, then you might well find that this practice leads you into a situation where you have to confront these experiences. This may not be pleasant, but can be, if you allow it, instructive, and possibly healing.

If, for whatever reason, you *do* find that working with a Demon Lover brings up problems that you find difficult to handle, then there are basically three strategies which can be brought up. The first is to perform a thorough Banishing of the area you are using for this practice (i.e., bedroom). Secondly, you can evoke the entity and confine it into a spirit trap such as a triangle, bottle, or crystal, and ritually re-bind it to your will. Thirdly, there is the option of reabsorption, which can be performed as a ritual or within the Liminal Gnosis. The simplest approach here is to take back the entities name, destroy any material base, visualize the emotions/ sensations/abilities you may have bestowed upon it as withdrawing back into your body and finally (and this *can* be difficult) denying it any sexual response or erotic association. Then, go and have a cold shower.

ILLUMINATION

> *"Illumination ... the inspiration, enlightenment and liberation resulting from success with these [Gnosis] methods."*
>
> — Peter J. Carroll, *Liber Null*

Illumination is the much-desired goal for which many thousands of people worldwide, have employed different psycho-technologies, and developed their own psychocosms. Illumination has also been linked with the use of LSD and similar drugs, and perhaps most mysteriously of all, it can occur seemingly spontaneously, to people who have no knowledge or expectation of it.

What characterizes an experience of illumination?

1. Unity — a fading of the self-other divide
2. Transcendence of space & time as barriers to experience
3. Positive sensations
4. A sense of the numinous
5. A sense of certitude — the "realness" of the experience
6. Paradoxical insights
7. Transience — the experience does not last
8. Resultant change in attitude and behavior.

What are the fruits of this experience — the insights, perceptions and messages brought back down to earth by the illuminate? Evolution of consciousness, by such means, could well be an important survival program — a way of going beyond the information given — a way of learning how to modify the human biosystem via the environment. Ilya Prigognine's theory of "dissipative structures" shows how the very instability of open systems allows them to be self-transforming. The basis of this idea is that the movement of energy through a system causes fluctuations within it. These fluctuations, if they reach a critical level (i.e., a catastrophe cusp point) develop novel interactions, until a new whole is produced. The system then reorganizes itself into a new "higher order" which is more integrated than the previous system, and requires a greater amount of energy to maintain itself, and is further disposed to future transformation. This can equally apply to neurological evolution, using a psycho-technology (ancient or modern) as the tool for change. The core stages of the process appear to be:

1. Change
2. Crisis
3. Transcendence
4. Transformation
5. Predisposition to further change.

It has long been understood that Numinous sexuality can trigger long-lasting Illuminations. Timothy Leary, for example, notes that the experience bliss states can often act as 'triggers' to an individual making a transformative journey. Such states of consciousness can arise at any time, as a byproduct of magical activity. In Tantric practice, such states are classed as achievements ('siddhas') which arise from one's continued practice, in their own time. Problems occur because some people, having heard about such intense states of consciousness, decide that they too *must* have such an experience, and rush off to seek it out, impatiently tossing aside practices and partners when they fail to live up to their wish for immediate gratification.

A bout of blissful sex, cannot of itself wipe out years of cultural conditioning, but it can be a spur for the desire to expand will and imagination in all regions of consciousness. It is not merely a case of replacing one set of self-beliefs and attitudes with another, but of allowing more flexibility and uncertainty into our lives. Surrendering oneself to the will of another person, to an unfamiliar state of consciousness, or otherwise 'letting go' of the world has a powerful transformative potential.

One approach to sex-magical illumination is for one partner to act as an seek "oracular realization" on a question via any preferred type of sexual play. Cut-up tapes may be used to provide layers of information. Whilst being pleasured for example, one partner may seek the 'answer' to a question or issue in whatever images, thoughts, feelings which arise during ritualized sex-play. He or She could for example, use magical glossolalia — mumbling (or screaming!) word-fragments and vowel sounds, until a coherent word or phrase is reached. Some magicians use this technique to obtain personalized 'words of power' which relate to the integration of their shadow-selves.

The power of sexual magic to bring about moments of illumination can also trigger the development of psychic abilities such as clairvoyance or clairaudience. One of the most effective (and enjoyable) ways of developing your psychic sensitivity is in sex-play with someone you care about. Astral projection, shared dreaming, and telepathic connections are also possible.

Finally, remember that for sexual magic, as much as any other aspect of magic, 'power' resides in you, rather than symbols, mantras, archetypes, deities, etc. Just as the power of magic resides within us, by the same token we must recognize our responsibility for how we go about wielding this power. The key to understanding sexual magic is that it is not so much about being "good" at sex-magic, but how the sexual magic you perform leads to self-change and development in *all* aspects of one's life.

FROM CHRISTOPHER S. HYATT, Ph.D.

TO LIE IS HUMAN
Not Getting Caught Is Divine

Introduced by Robert Anton Wilson

Take a tour of the prison erected by the lies that society tells you…and the lies you tell yourself. Then, learn the tools to tunnel out…

"Is it possible to use language to undo the hallucinations created by language? …a few heroic efforts seem able to jolt readers awake… to transcend words."
— Robert Anton Wilson

SEX MAGICK, TANTRA & TAROT
The Way of the Secret Lover

With Lon Milo DuQuette
Illustrated by David P. Wilson

A wealth of practical and passionate Tantric techniques utilizing the Archetypal images of the Tarot. Nothing is held back. All methods are explicit and clearly described.

"Each of us has a Guardian Angel — a companion and lover who waits just behind the images that flood our minds during sleep or reverie."

FROM CHRISTOPHER S. HYATT, Pʜ.D.

RADICAL UNDOING
The Complete Course for Undoing Yourself

For the first time on DVD, these effective and powerful Tantric methods help you to open your Chakras and release your Kundalini energy. With practice you will learn to harness this powerful sexual energy and experience *The Ultimate Orgasm.*

ENERGIZED HYPNOSIS

With Calvin Iwema, M.A.

Energized Hypnosis is a *breakthrough* program of DVDs, CDs, booklets and a "non-book" for gaining personal power, peace of mind and enlightenment. The techniques of **Energized Hypnosis** were developed many years ago by Dr. Christopher Hyatt and Dr. Israel Regardie, but have remained "in the closet"...until now.